Collins Illustrated Guide to

FUJIAN

Caroline Courtauld

COLLINS

8 Grafton Street, London W1

1988

William Collins Sons & Co. Ltd
London • Glasgow • Sydney • Auckland
Toronto • Johannesburg

British Library Cataloguing in Publication Data

Collins Illustrated Guide to Fujian — (China Guides Series)
1. Fujian Province (China) — Description and Travel — Guide-books
I. Series
915.1'2'45   DS793.F8

ISBN 0-00-215265-7

Series Editors: May Holdsworth and Jill Hunt
Picture Editor: Ingrid Morejohn
Contributing Editor: Peter Fredenburg

Photography by Caroline Courtauld (3, 10−11, 14, 28−9, 32, 36, 44−5, 60, 64, 73, 80, 84−5, 98, 110−1, 118−9, 123, 134); Rebecca Lee (48, 52, 102−3); Carolyn Watts (25, 65); Ingrid Morejohn (77); Wang Gang Feng (7, 17, 88, 96, 119, 138); David Lung (130−1); and Jardine, Matheson and Co., Limited (57)

Cover photographs by Wang Gang Feng (front) and Rebecca Lee (back)

The Guidebook Company wishes to express special thanks to China Travel Service of Fujian Province and the Fujian Tourism Bureau for all their help; and to the Urban Council of Hong Kong for arranging the picture on page 77.

Design by Rican Design Associates

Printed in Hong Kong

Contents

Names and Addresses

In this book addresses are given in *Pinyin. Dajie* is a main thoroughfare; *lu* is a road and *jie* is a street; *xiang* is a lane or alley. To help visitors getting about on their own, names of hotels and restaurants are given in Chinese characters in the text. while names of all the sights, shops and other places described in the book are given in Chinese characters either in the Useful Addresses section or in the Index of Places.

Fujian Province

Fujian Province has a tremendous amount to teach the visitor about China both ancient and modern. Its history reaches back over 2,000 years, and today the province exemplifies China's 'Open Door' policy. Fujianese people are said to epitomise Chinese entrepreneurial skills — in particular in their aptitude for all sorts of trading. This is as evident in the bustling markets of Xiamen as in the business empires built all over Southeast Asia by Fujianese emigrants. The province is the ancestral home of about one-third of the world's overseas Chinese (approximately 20 million) — a direct consequence of its coastal position and long seafaring tradition (see page 24). Its sons and daughters from far away continue to make contributions towards their home province, and the role of *huaqiao* (overseas Chinese) features prominently in Fujian's development plans.

Fujian is lozenge-shaped — some 120,000 square kilometres (46,000 square miles) in area (about the size of England), and nearly all of it is beautiful and much of it covered by subtropical vegetation.

To the north, west and south mountains form its border, while to the east the province looks some 160 kilometres (100 miles) across the straits to Taiwan. Fujian's coastline is more twisted and complex than the carved dragons that can be seen encircling temple pillars throughout the province. Only extending about 500 kilometres (310 miles) as the crow flies, the coastline in fact meanders in and out and around covering over 3,000 kilometres (1,800 miles). The 1,000 or so offshore islands provide not only outstanding fishing grounds — there are said to be more than 600 varieties of fish readily available — but also help to form the excellent natural harbours which have always played a vital role in the life of the province. Fuzhou, Quanzhou and Xiamen are the most important of these, but there are dozens more. The proximity to Taiwan is another geographic factor that has exerted a powerful influence on Fujian. Even before the arrival of Generalissimo Chiang Kai-shek and his Guomindang (Nationalist) followers in 1949, the majority of the people in Taiwan were of Fujianese extraction. In addition to Mandarin of course, the same local dialect is spoken on both sides of the straits. Active trade between the two economies has taken place even when frowned on by the authorities; relatives somehow manage to visit one another and many even cross from Taiwan to die in their motherland.

Fujian's climate is subtropical maritime, with hot and sticky summers, cool and pleasant autumns and winters. Plentiful rainfall and the backdrop of hills and mountains have produced rivers short and swift. Power is harnessed on the rivers by a large number of hydro-electric schemes which contribute to the province's annual generating capacity of 32 billion kilowatt hours, the highest in southeast China.

The province is rich in natural resources, too. More than 100 types of minerals are mined, including tungsten, iron, aluminium and copper. Some 40 percent of the province is covered in forest — the highest percentage in China — and it is actively exploited. Only some 20 percent of Fujian's land area is suitable for agriculture, but that portion is highly fertile, in particular the area encompassing Xiamen, Zhangzhou, Quanzhou and the 16 counties under their jurisdiction.

The history of Fujian is long. Some say that it was the first emperor of China, during the Qin Dynasty (221—207 BC), who initiated the prefecture of Fujian. Certainly by the sixth century Fujian was a distinct unit in China's administrative structure, the city of Fuzhou had been founded and the impact of Fujian's geographic position was evident. In the Tang Dynasty (608—907) Quanzhou was reputedly host to several hundred thousand foreign merchants, who called the city 'Zaytun'. At the height of its importance (during the Yuan Dynasty 1279—1368), it is thought to have been second only to Alexandria in port traffic. Indeed, Marco Polo, who spent some time there prior to leaving China for the last time, referred to Quanzhou as the 'Alexandria of the East'.

The destiny of the province continued to be linked with the sea. As overseas trade diminished during the late Ming Dynasty — a period when China shrank from contact with the outside world — the interests of the province were focused inward and on national politics. Under the leadership of General Zheng Chenggong (named Koxinga by the Europeans) Fujian became the last stronghold of the Ming Dynasty against the advancing Manchus. But some 200 years later, the coming of foreign trade changed Fujian's fortunes again. The Treaty of Nanking, signed with the British in 1842, marked the end of the first Opium War and named Fuzhou (Foochow) and Xiamen (Amoy) as two of the five Treaty Ports opened to foreign trade.

Today, having suffered another period of closure to the outside world from the 1950s to the late 1970s, Fujian is 'open' again. Since the initiation of China's 'Four Modernizations' policy in 1978, Fujian's economic development has been rapid. The province's geographic advantages, financial infusions from overseas compatriots and the entrepreneurial attitudes of its people have been supplemented by the policies and encouragement of the central and provincial governments. The present governor of Fujian, Hu Ping, summed it up well: 'The history of Fujian proves that the economy prospers when it is opened and stagnates when it is closed.' In 1981, one of China's five Special Economic Zones was established at Xiamen, and Fuzhou was also granted special economic privileges to attract foreign investment and know-how. Although Fujian's population of 26 million only accounts for some 2.5 percent of China's total, its industrial production and manufactured exports represent a much larger proportion of the national total. The province's major industrial ventures include steel rolling and production of high-quality television sets and cassette tape-recorders. As in other parts of China, economic development has certainly not been easy; but the visitor who has seen other provinces is struck by the evidence of commercial activity in town and countryside alike.

Tremendous efforts have been made in Fujian in recent years to attract the foreign visitor both on business and pleasure. One can travel independently in Fujian without feeling like a processed tourist. There is plenty of scope for exploration and surprise whether you are in the back streets of Gulangyu or in the misty recesses of Wuyi Mountain. The province's ravishing scenery, mountains and seascapes; its exciting and varied cultural scene; outstanding monuments and, not least, its 'Min' cuisine, offer a cornucopia of pleasures for the visitor.

Getting To and Around Fujian

By Air

Fuzhou and Xiamen can be reached by a limited number of regional international services and from a number of points within China.

CAAC (Civil Aviation Administration of China) is the only airline flying to Fuzhou, with departures from Hong Kong daily except Sunday and taking one hour 10 minutes.

Hong Kong's Dragon Airlines (Dragonair) makes the one-hour flight from Hong Kong to Xiamen on Wednesday and Saturday. CAAC flights on the same route are daily except Saturday, with the Friday flight stopping in Guangzhou.

Early afternoon flights from Manila to Xiamen are operated Monday, Wednesday and Saturday by Philippine Airlines with returns the following day. CAAC makes the trip on Thursday. Flight duration is two hours 15 minutes. There is one charter every three weeks from Singapore.

Within China, scheduled flights connect Fuzhou with Beijing, Guangzhou, Hangzhou, Hefei, Nanchang, Nanjing, Shanghai and Wuhan.

Domestic services to Xiamen are operated from Beijing, Guangzhou, Guilin, Hangzhou, Nanchang, Shanghai and Xi'an.

Fuzhou Airport is seven kilometres (four miles) south of the city. Xiamen International Airport is 12 kilometres (seven miles) north of town, at the island end of the causeway.

By Bus

Fuzhou, Xiamen and Quanzhou can be reached by semi-direct, air-conditioned buses from Hong Kong. Buses depart from various locations in Hong Kong, the most convenient for tourists being the old Macau Ferry terminal. Across the border, in Shenzhen, passengers transfer to another bus for the remainder of the journey. Reservations can be made through the Hua Min Tourism Company, Ltd, which is operated by Fujian Province and maintains an office in Hong Kong (see Useful Addresses on page 137).

The bus to Fuzhou is run by Ka Tai Trading Company and departs at 8.30 am daily. The trip takes 22 hours and costs Rmb72. The buses to Xiamen and Quanzhou are operated by Fujian Tourist Bus Company Ltd, and depart at 7 am arriving in Xiamen 20 hours later and costing Rmb55; Quanzhou is reached in 22 hours and the fare is Rmb62.

A similar daily bus service operated by CITS to Fuzhou, Xiamen, Quanzhou and Zhangzhou is closed to foreigners for lack of proper immigration facilities at the crossing.

There are buses from Guangzhou to Fuzhou and Xiamen.

By Boat

The *Jimei* and the *Gulangyu* sail from Hong Kong to Xiamen Tuesday and Friday respectively. No fewer than six classes of passage range in price from Rmb129 to Rmb357 (slightly more if booked through CITS), with the two top classes comfortable enough to satisfy just about anyone. The 12.30 pm departure provides a close look at the hustle and bustle of Hong Kong harbour. Arrival in Xiamen 19 hours later coincides with the daily departure of the local fishing boats. The *Jimei* leaves for Hong Kong on Friday, and the *Gulangyu* on Tuesday, with both departures at 3 pm.

A third boat, the *Maoxin*, runs from Fuzhou to Shanghai every five days.

By Train

Because the trunk lines connecting Beijing and Shanghai pass well inland of Fujian, the province is a bit out of the way by rail, restricting the number of trains serving the province. Nevertheless, express trains arrive in Fuzhou daily from Beijing, Hangzhou, Nanchang and Guangzhou. Xiamen can be reached from Shanghai and Nanjing.

General Information for Travellers

Visas

Everyone must get a visa to go to China, but this is usually an easy, trouble-free process. Tourists travelling in a group are listed on a single group visa — a special document listing all members of the group — which is issued in advance to tour organizers. Individual passports of people travelling on a group visa will not be stamped unless specifically requested.

Tourist visas for individual travellers (those who are not travelling in a group) can be obtained directly through Chinese embassies and consulates, although some embassies are more enthusiastic about issuing them than others. Certain travel agents and tour operators around the world can arrange individual visas for their clients. It is

simplest in Hong Kong, where there are a large number of travel agents handling visa applications. Just one passport photograph and a completed application form are necessary.

Visa fees vary considerably, depending on the source of the visa, and on the time taken to get it. In Hong Kong, for instance, some travel agents can get you a tourist visa in a few hours, but it may cost around US$30 for one valid for three months, while a one-month visa which takes 48 hours to obtain might cost just US$7.

The visa gives you automatic entry to all China's open cities and areas (there were 436 in 1987).

Customs

A customs declaration form must be filled out by each visitor upon entry. On this document you are required to list valuable possessions such as tape recorders, cameras, watches, jewellery etc, and which must be taken out with you when you leave, as well as foreign currency. The carbon copy of this form will be returned to you and it must be produced at customs for inspection on departure from China.

Any antique bought for export should bear a brown or red wax seal, which tells customs officials that it may be taken out of the country, so be sure to keep the seal on. It is also advisable to keep all sales receipts.

Four bottles of alcohol, three cartons of cigarettes, unlimited film and unlimited medicines for personal use may be taken in. Firearms and dangerous drugs are strictly forbidden. It is also illegal to acquire Chinese money abroad and take it in.

Money

Chinese Currency The Chinese currency, which is sometimes referred to as Renminbi or Rmb, meaning 'people's currency', is denominated in *yuan* which are each divided into 10 *jiao*, colloquially called *mao*. Each *jiao* is, in turn, divided into 10 *fen*. There are large notes for 100, 50, 10, 5, 2 and 1 *yuan*, small notes for 5, 2 and 1 *jiao*, and coins for 5, 2 and 1 *fen*.

Currency Certificates Foreign Exchange Certificates (FEC) were introduced in 1980. They were designed to be used instead of Renminbi by foreign visitors for payment in hotels, Friendship Stores, at trade fairs, and for airline tickets, international phone calls, parcel post, etc. In practice, however, FEC quickly became a sought-after form of payment anywhere, and a black market developed between the two currencies. In September 1986, the Chinese government announced its intention of phasing out FECs, but implementation seems to have been indefinitely postponed, and FECs remain in circulation.

FEC and Rmb may be reconverted into foreign currency or taken out when you leave China, but it is impossible to change them abroad.

Foreign Currency There is no limit to the amount of foreign currency you may bring into China. It is advisable to keep your exchange vouchers as the bank may demand to see them when you convert Chinese currency back into foreign currency on leaving China.

All the major freely negotiable currencies can be exchanged at branches of the Bank of China, in hotels and stores.

Cheques and Credit Cards All the usual American, European and Japanese travellers cheques are acceptable. Credit cards may be used in a limited number of Friendship Stores, hotels and banks, and you should check with your credit card company or bank before you rely on this form of payment for your purchases. Personal cheques are sometimes taken in return for goods which are shipped after the cheque is cleared.

Tipping Tipping was forbidden in China, but the practice has made a reappearance in recent years. Although the current policy is unclear, drivers and other tourism staff in particular have been accepting tips for some time, especially at those destinations most regularly visited by tourists.

Travel Agencies

There are a number of State-owned corporations which handle foreign visitors to China, but the largest is CITS (China International Travel Service). Other large organizations providing similar services are CTS (China Travel Service) and CYTS (China Youth Travel Service).

CITS offers a comprehensive service covering accommodation, transport, food, sightseeing, interpreters and special visits to schools, hospitals, factories and other places foreigners might be interested to see. It also provides services such as ticket sales for walk-in customers.

Climate and Clothing

Fujian has a moist subtropical climate. The weather is dominated by a hot, wet monsoon in autumn but largely shielded by mountains from the cold winds blowing from Siberia in winter.

January and February are the coolest months. Temperatures in Fuzhou average 12.5°C (55°F), with an average high of 15°C (59°F) by day and a low of 7°C (45°F) at night. Cities further south and right on the coast, such as Xiamen and Quanzhou, are warmer by about 2°C

(4°F) with less daily fluctuations, but places further inland and at higher elevations can be unpredictable and considerably cooler. Temperatures as low as −4°C (25°F) are sometimes recorded at Wuyi.

Visitors should bear in mind that even in the coastal cities the temperatures can drop close to freezing and that the humidity can drive a chill right to the bone. Heating is rare south of the Yangzi River, making layered clothing a good idea. A warm sweater and a jacket are recommended. Visitors to Wuyi may also want gloves and a hat. Also, thermal underwear weighs little but takes the sting out of an unexpectedly cold snap.

July and August are uniformly hot, with temperatures in Fuzhou averaging 28.5°C (83°F). The average high is 33°C (91°F) and the average low is 25°C (77°F). Again, Xiamen and Quanzhou are slightly milder, but even Xiamen records temperatures as high as 36°C (97°F). Light cotton clothing is in order. Be warned that baring too much skin invites not only sunburn but also stares of astonishing frankness.

In the period just before the hot weather, an umbrella is essential, as the rainy season starts in March in the north — April or May in the south — and continues through June. During this period, rain (usually drizzle) falls on more days than not. The farther inland one travels, the wetter it gets. Xiamen, with about 110 centimetres (43 inches) of rain a year, is somewhat drier than Fuzhou, which receives about 20 percent more. Wuyi receives fully 219 centimetres (85 inches), 60 percent of which falls from March to June.

The typhoon season centres on August and September but begins a month earlier in the south and extends a month later in the north. The season is defined by the threat — rather than the actual presence — of typhoons; usually the weather is fine. Still, the south in particular can be slammed by perhaps four or five big storms in a season.

Though there is no time of year to avoid Fujian absolutely, spring (March-May) and autumn (September-December) are the best times to go. In April and November, the average temperature is about 19°C (66°F), with the daytime high a perfect 22°C (72°F) and the night-time low a very comfortable 16°C (61°F).

Fujian Food

Fujian or Min cooking is one of eight 'notable styles' in Chinese cuisine. As Fujian is a coastal province, emphasis is on fish and shellfish. The dishes are fresh and light, often a little sweet as they are flavoured with rice or grain wine. And each area has its own speciality.

In Fuzhou, the provincial capital, the local delicacy is a type of freshwater mussel (*haibang*), which is only found at the mouth of the

Min River nearby and 7,000 miles away in Venice, Italy. The shell is
semi-circular, the shape of an oyster, with the texture and colouring
nearly that of a mussel. It is rare and therefore expensive. The mussels
are not available in the markets: the daily catch is delivered to the
tourist hotels and better restaurants. Seeking out a meal of freshwater
mussel is certainly worth the effort. Its tender white flesh has a delicate
flavour, and it is either served in a broth or gently sautéed in local wine
with green pepper and cucumber. Another of Fuzhou's famous dishes
is 'Buddha jumping over the wall' (Fo Tiao Qiang), a concoction of
seafood, mutton, pork, chicken and duck sealed in a terracotta pot
(the shape of a ginger jar). Reputedly, its aroma enticed Buddha into
jumping over a wall to find the source.

The province is also famous for its mushrooms. They are grown on
Wuyi Mountain and some 150 kilometres (93 miles) north of Fuzhou,
where the She minority people live. The She are famous for their
'Fragrant Mushrooms', which they cultivate in sheds on specially
tailored posts, each about a foot long. These contraptions stand at an
angle, rather like slightly drunk soldiers. The She people also grow
mushrooms in the stubble of the paddy fields after harvest. The spores
are fertilized, covered in rice straw and quickly brought to maturity.
Another favourite type of local mushroom is the small golden variety
(*jingu*). This is either used in soups or sautéed and served cold,
sprinkled with a little sesame oil.

Quanzhou and Zhangzhou cuisine is centred on oysters, razor fish
and many types of crustacea. The wide muddy-banked Jin and Jiulong
Rivers offer such creatures a perfect habitat. Small oysters are put into
duck-egg omelettes or deep fried with chilli. (The food in the south of
the province is often seasoned with chilli.) Zhangzhou boasts its own
fish, the Lou, found only in the lower reaches of the Jiulong River. It
has firm flesh and a delicate flavour. Of all the crustacea available in
the province, perhaps the most delicious and certainly the most widely
available is crab. Whether it is simply steamed with ginger or prepared
in an elaborate way, it will be sweet and tender.

Throughout the province one is able to sample truly delicious
noodles. Again, each area has its own special kind, some a little
thinner or thicker than others, but the ingredient that makes Fujian
noodles so special is fish. Both shellfish and flat fish are used,
sometimes with vegetables, sometimes not, and the end result is
mouth-watering.

It is difficult to have a bad meal in Fujian, since the raw materials
are excellent. The food is prepared and presented with great style and
the Fujianese sensibly shy away from meat as they do not, by and
large, farm animals. It must be hoped that the influx of foreign visitors
who have different eating habits will do nothing to destroy the superb
Min Cuisine.

← To Nanping & Wuyi

To Snow Peak Temple →

● Lin Zexu Memorial Hall

Beida Lu

Bayiqi Lu

West Lake Park ●

West Lake Guesthouse

● Minjiang

Kaiyuan Temple
●

Juchunyuan Resta

●
Zoo

Qiaolia

Friendship St

Jinshan Temple
●

Dongjiekou Department Store ●

White Pagoda ●

Y

Dongda Lu

● Ebony Pagoda

Xichan Temple
●

Wu Shan

Gongye Lu

Long-distance Bus Station

●

N A N

To Yongtai →

A

N

Fuzhou

- Chongfu Temple
- Railway Station
- East Railway Station
- Liuyi Lu
- Lianjiang Lu
- CAAC Booking Office
- Taijiang Lu
- Aofeng Lu
- ng Department Store
- Min River
- ISLAND
- Mawei
- Luoxing Pagoda •
- Wulong River

Fuzhou

Fujian's capital, Fuzhou, has grown up on both banks of the Min River (Minjiang) and has a population of some 700,000. It is a well laid out city, with many trees, some of which are over 900 years old. The tree planting was initiated by an enlightened Song-Dynasty governor and gave rise to Fuzhou's second name, 'Banyan City'.

The topography of Fuzhou is interesting: three hills dominate the city, a fourth lies to the east. A hot spring stream runs from north to south under the eastern side of the city. The southern section of Fuzhou across the Min River is in fact a lozenge-shaped island between the Min and Wulong Rivers.

The city was founded in the sixth century, and reputedly gained its present name during the eighth century. By the time of the Five Dynasties (907−60), Fuzhou had become the capital of an autonomous region called Min (Fujian is still sometimes referred to as 'Min') with a king at its helm. Under the Song it became a prosperous trading base. The cult of Manichaeism, a strange religion founded in third-century Persia, apparently had a strong following here during the Song and Yuan Dynasties, presumably due to the large numbers of foreign merchants then visiting Fuzhou.

The great eunuch admiral Zheng He made Fuzhou his final port of call before embarking on his seven trips of exploration (1405−33) to the Indian Ocean. The sight of his 62 junks carrying 28,000 men sailing up the Min River must have been awe-inspiring. China's short age of exploration died with the admiral in 1435.

Fuzhou, as the capital of a province isolated from the rest of China by mountains and offering escape by sea, has played host to several dignitaries on the run. Two imperial princes and loyalists of the Southern Song Dynasty retreated to Fujian in 1276, but held out just three years before Kublai Khan and his Mongol supporters brought the whole of China together under the Yuan Dynasty. Three-hundred-and-sixty-nine years later, after the Manchu had gained control of the north of China and established the Qing Dynasty in 1644, Fujian became the last stronghold of the remnants of the Ming Dynasty. Gradually the loyal Ming troops led by General Zheng Chenggong (Koxinga) were pushed further south to Xiamen. When they were finally beaten in 1659, General Zheng and his troops retreated to Taiwan. As soon as the Manchu had control of Fuzhou they fortified the city and installed a large garrison.

Fuzhou continued to prosper as a port and market town under the Qing and eventually attracted the attention of European merchants in the 18th century. China resisted foreign contact but in 1840 relations between the inward-looking Chinese Empire and the impatient Europeans boiled over briefly in the first Opium War. This resulted in the signing between China and Britain of the Treaty of Nanking, which named Fuzhou (Foochow) as one of the five Treaty Ports to be opened to foreign traders. From 1861 European traders settled in Fuzhou, building their houses on the south bank of the Min River. In the 1880s the French began to cause the Qing government problems on several fronts, based on their desire for more access to trade in China and her suzerain states. The French already controlled Cochin China (South Vietnam) and now began a northward push. They invaded the Pescadores and Taiwan, sailed up and blockaded the Yangzi (Yangtse) River, preventing the annual tribute ships from reaching Beijing and in 1884 destroyed the newly-built Chinese fleet at Fuzhou.

During the Sino-Japanese War (1937—45) Fuzhou was bombed, blockaded and occasionally occupied by the Japanese. By the time the Japanese threat was finally quelled China was embroiled in an internal struggle. Chiang Kai-shek and his Nationalist troops were pushed south by the advancing Mao Zedong and the communists. Just as it had been the last stronghold under the Ming in 1644, Fujian became the final mainland base for the Nationalists. On 17 August 1948 Fuzhou fell to the communists.

Hotels in Fuzhou

Fujian Foreign Trade Centre Hotel (Fujian Waimao Zhongxin Jiudian)
14 Wusi Lu
tel. 550154
tlx. 92158
fax. 550358

福建外贸中心酒店
五四路14号

75 double (Rmb90) and 60 twin (Rmb110) rooms, 30 suites (Rmb190—200). Banquet hall (max. 300), Fujianese, Cantonese and Western restaurants; secretarial and conference facilities; hairdresser; disco; hot springs; swimming pool (from 1988). (Amex, MasterCard, Visa, Nanyang Commercial Bank)

Opened in 1986, the FTC Hotel offers the best accommodation of the three new hotels in Fuzhou and is conveniently located in the city's commercial area. The lobby drips with brilliant lighting and marble. The well-stocked shop sells, among other things, the much sought-after silk vests, but Kodak film sells for Rmb15.60 here as opposed to Rmb10 in the Minjiang across the street.

Chinese Emigration

Lynn Pan

It was on the southern coasts of Fujjian that the story of the Chinese Diaspora truly began. A mountainous, coastal province, Fujian offered a hard life to the rice farmer, but ample opportunities to the maritime trader. The Fujianese have been settling in the countries of Southeast Asia since the end of the Song Dynasty, and now they constitute between a third to a half of all the overseas Chinese. Down the centuries son and nephew had followed father or uncle to Nanyang, 'the southern seas', sharing their newfound prosperity with their ancestral villages in the form of remittances, donations and investments in modern commercial undertakings. It was with the expectation that Fujian's emigrant sons would continue to bankroll projects in their hometowns that the current Chinese regime established the Xiamen SEZ.

For reasons of national security, overseas trade and emigration was banned by imperial decree during much of the Ming and Qing Dynasties, but even before the prohibition was lifted in 1894, the tide of an eastward and southward movement of pioneer settlers had set in. The eastward movement laid the foundations of Chinese settlements in nearby Formosa (Taiwan), an island the Chinese annals had described as 'Land of the Eastern Savages'. Fishermen, pirates, traders and maritime adventurers from the seaboard cities of Fujian were among the first Chinese to frequent the Taiwan Straits; and, because those who went abroad ran the risk of being beheaded upon their return, many simply decided to make Taiwan their home.

Meanwhile, trade routes had opened from the Fujian seaboard to the Philippines, British Malacca (in Malaya), and the Dutch East Indies (modern Indonesia). These paved the way for yet another great wave of migration. Sailing with the 'trade winds', it took only three days for an ocean-going junk from the Fujian coast to reach Manila, a thriving entrepot of the Spanish galleon trade to the New World. Vast quantities of Mexican silver streamed into China via Manila to pay for the silks and porcelain of China, and it was the natives of southern Fujian who handled the eastern end of the galleon trade.

The story of the Fujianese immigrants in Manila is with minor variations the story of the overseas Chinese in many communities. They clustered in their own quarter — the Parian, an early example of Chinatown. They were hamstrung by discriminatory taxes and irksome restrictions. They were massacred in their thousands and periodically expelled. They dominated economic life; they enriched themselves on the opium and gambling licensed monopolies; and their families abounded in spectacular rags-to-riches stories. Almost entirely male, they intermarried with local women and converted to Catholicism, giving rise to Chinese *mestizos* — a class of people of mixed Filipino and Chinese origin — who came to occupy a crucial place in national life. The earliest known ancestor of no less a personage than the poet and patriot José Rizal, the Philippines' pre-eminent national hero, was a 17th-century Chinese migrant from Fujian Province.

Chinese emigration to Southeast Asia increased in the wake of the famous naval expeditions of Admiral Zheng He to the Indian Ocean in the early 15th century. Glorified in the folklore of the overseas Chinese, Zheng He has been revered as a deity in Malacca, Thailand, Java, and other Southeast Asian countries for centuries. Though not a native of Fujian himself, Zheng He commanded fleets of Fujianese crewmen.

From about the middle of the 19th century, the waves of Chinese emigration from the south China coast grew into a flood with the coolie trade, an operation scarcely distinguishable from the African slave trade. Until it was superseded by Canton, Macau and Hong Kong, Amoy (Xiamen) was the first Chinese port to bristle with barracoons, coolie crimps, and Western clippers and emigration agents arranging for the shipment of vast numbers of indentured labourers to the United States, Cuba, Peru, and the furthest corners of the British Empire.

One British colony to which the southern Fujianese migrated in large numbers was the Straits Settlements (Singapore, Penang and Malacca) and today Hokkiens (the pronunciation of the name 'Fujian' in the dialect of the Amoy hinterland) are a force of great consequence in these places. The earliest immigrants intermarried with Malay women and evolved a culture and cuisine of their own. Called Straits Chinese, or Babas, these settlers were a Hokkien-Malay hybrid, speaking a *patois* based on Malay but laced with many words of Hokkien origin.

Words of Fujian origin have entered the vocabulary of not just Malay, but also English and Tagalog, the national language of the Philippines. At the same time as it exported people, Fujian exported words: 'satin' comes from Zaytun, the predecessor of Quanzhou; 'tea' from the Amoy word *te*; while 'junk' is derived from the Malay approximation of the Amoy pronunciation of *chuan*, the Chinese word for ship. It is perhaps symbolic of the character of overseas Chinese activity that a fifth of the Hokkien-Chinese contributions to Tagalog consist of the names of foods and culinary terms, while another 18 percent relates to callings or professions.

**Hot Spring Hotel
(Wenquan Dasha)**
Wusi Lu (Middle
section)
tel. 551818
tlx. 92180,
fax. 535150
Cable 8426

温泉大厦
五四路中段

*311 double rooms (Rmb120−40) and suites
(Rmb180−1,200). Business centre; banquet
and function rooms (max. 1,200); Chinese and
Western restaurants; gymnasium and sauna;
bowling; disco; tennis courts and swimming
pool will be added in 1987. (Amex,
MasterCard, Visa, Federal)*

A nicely designed new hotel with a vast, 15-
floor high atrium lobby, along one wall of
which glass lifts go up and down. The ground
floor is made up of two lakes and islands, one
of which is graced by a white grand piano!
Two deluxe Chinese restaurants — the Ming
Palace and Lychee Village — serve Fujianese
and Cantonese fare, including *dim sum*
specialities in the latter. The bedrooms are
pleasant and well-equipped and even have
hairdryers in all the bathrooms.

Reservations may be made direct or
through Pearl International Hotels, Room 605
Tower B, Mandarin Plaza, Tsimshatsui East,
Kowloon, Hong Kong (tel. 3-692623 and
tlx. 49350).

**East Lake Guesthouse
(Donghu Binguan)**
44 Dongda Lu
tel. 557755
tlx. 92171,
fax. 55519

东湖宾馆
东大路44号

*174 rooms including 6 suites, Rmb50−350.
Banqueting and conference facilities;
secretarial services; disco; two Cantonese and
one Fujianese restaurants, Western restaurant-
cum-coffee shop; hot springs. (Amex,
MasterCard, Visa, Federal)*

A joint-venture hotel with Hong Kong
partners, this guesthouse is run by CITS. The
bedrooms, though laid with rather ill-chosen
pale carpets that all too clearly show up signs
of wear, are otherwise well decorated. The
Jade Garden Restaurant (Cuiyuan Gong)
serves excellent Fujianese cuisine.

**West Lake Hotel
(Xihu Binguan)**
Hubin Lu
tel. 557008
tlx. 92154

西湖宾馆
湖滨路

No. 6 Building: 15 single (Rmb38) and 23 double (Rmb62) rooms. Fujianese restaurant and Western-style coffee shop; banqueting facilities; secretarial services in Chinese only; garden and a brand-new all-weather tennis court with sports equipment for hire

Set in an enormous garden stocked with lovely trees and potted shrubs (although some Disney World-type 'animals' are now to be seen 'gambolling' through the grounds), this hotel stands beside the West Lake. The No. 6 Building accepts foreign guests and offers comfortable rooms, reasonable everyday meals and excellent banquet food. A high-rise building is under construction and will be added to the complex in 1988.

Minjiang Hotel
Wusi Lu
tel. 557895
tlx. 92146,
fax. 551489
Cable 8117

闽江饭店
五四路

400 rooms, Rmb59 for single, Rmb70 for standard double, Rmb150—302 for suites. Fujianese, Jiangsu and Cantonese restaurants and Western restaurant; banqueting facilities; secretarial services; disco. (Amex, Diners Club, MasterCard, Visa)

Neither the accommodation nor the service in this hotel is especially noteworthy, and waiting for lifts can be an exercise in patience. The ground-floor Fujianese and Jiangsu restaurant is recommended, and a good Western breakfast is served on the 15th floor. An endless supply of hot springs water is piped to the rooms.

Yushan Hotel
Gutian Lu
tel. 551668
tlx. 92115
Cable 8886

于山饭店
古田路

190 beds, Rmb70 for standard double, some rooms with 5-bed accommodation available for Rmb10 per head. Banqueting facilities

This is an old-style hotel with rooms distributed in several buildings. These are set in a nice garden. The hotel is run by Fuzhou Municipality and its clientele is made up of government officials and foreign visitors.

Overseas Chinese Mansion (Huaqiao Dasha)
Wusi Lu
tel. 557603
tlx. 92123

华侨大厦
五四路

175 rooms, standard double Rmb28—89 for overseas Chinese and Rmb40—118 for foreign guests. Some triple-bed accommodation available. Banquet rooms; hot spring bathwater; Chinese and Western restaurants. (Amex, Diners Club, MasterCard, Federal, Nanyang Commercial Bank)

In mid-1987 this hotel was under renovation and resembled a building site, but the refurbishment plans sounded promising. China Travel Service's office is located here. The second-floor restaurant, Yaochi Canting, located in a separated building to the main wing, is recommended.

Qiaolian Mansion
Wuyi Bei Lu
tel. 57858
Cable 8499

侨联大厦
五一北路

90 rooms, about half available to foreign visitors (Rmb36—70 for double). Chinese restaurants, banquet rooms

Run by the Overseas Association, this old-fashioned hotel largely caters to Chinese guests but will also accept foreign visitors.

Restaurants in Fuzhou

Fuzhou Restaurant (Fuzhou Da Jiujia)
36 Dongda Lu
tel. 551396

福州大酒家
东大路36号

One of the most renowned restaurants in the city, the Fuzhou specializes in seafood prepared by two chefs who have won a national prize for their dishes and who cooked for President Ronald Reagan in Beijing. Sadly the restaurant has been recently smartened up and no longer retains the bistro atmosphere it once had. The large dining room on the first floor tends to be regularly used for wedding receptions. There are also several nicely decorated banquet rooms. The 'flattened prawns' and crab and egg stew are delicious.

Little Bridge Fuzhou Cuisine Market
tel. 59239

小桥风味小吃市场

This restaurant is part of a new shopping complex housed in an old-style building beside the canal. The shops downstairs are set up like an antique market. The restaurant on the upper floor serves a range of 'little delicacies' (*dim sum*), for example shark's fin marinated in vinegar, garlic and sugar and served cold, and glutinous rice balls rolled in chopped nuts and sugar, as well as a variety of noodle dishes. Open 7 am−midnight.

Juchunyuan
130 Bayiqi Bei Lu
tel. 553038

聚春园
八一七北路130号

Established in 1877, this restaurant has a long tradition of serving Fujianese cuisine and is where the famous dish 'Buddha jumping over the wall' is said to have originated. The large restaurant with a capacity for 500 guests is housed in an attractively decorated three-storey building.

Beijing Restaurant (Beijing Fanzhuang)
12 Dongda Lu
tel. 32334

北京饭庄
东大路12号

You can taste both Fujianese food and the widely popular Beijing duck here. The ducks are sent down from the capital. This flourishing restaurant can seat 200.

Chongqing Restaurant
105 Bayiqi Bei Lu
tel. 550615

重庆饭店
八一七北路105号

A cooperative established by two provincial governments, the Chongqing provides both Fujianese dishes and typically spicy Sichuanese fare.

Weizhongwei
Bayiqi Bei Lu

味中味
八一七北路

This great cavern of a *dim sum* restaurant is arranged in stalls, so as you go in you look down the signs and decide whether you want noodles, *jiaozi* (dumplings) or prefer to choose from great steamers filled with breads, and individual pots of soup. Even if you are not brave or not hungry enough, it is well worth just wandering around to watch the many regional delicacies being prepared under one, fine old roof.

Arts and Crafts in Fuzhou

Fuzhou presents a cornucopia of arts and crafts. In the realm of performing arts, there are many local opera groups; perhaps the best known is the Min (Fuzhou) Opera Troupe, who perform every night and are well worth tracking down. The majority of the opera plots are from famous historical tales, and their dramatic content is high — ideal if one does not understand the language. Min opera is little different to its Beijing equivalent except for the use of the Fuzhou dialect, the extra flutes and strings in the orchestra and the softer and more melodious singing.

Then there are the 'Three Handicraft Treasures of Fuzhou' — stone carving, lacquerware and cork sculpting, but that is just the tip of the iceberg. To make life easier for the visitor, however, the **Fuzhou Carving Arts and Crafts Factory** (Liuyi Lu) produces stone, wood, ivory and shell carving under one roof. Shoushan stone is quarried some 40 kilometres (25 miles) northwest of Fuzhou. The carving of Shoushan stone has a long history, as evidenced by a piece depicting two reclining pigs that was recently unearthed from a Southern-Dynasties (420–589) tomb. During the Ming and early Qing Dynasties Shoushan carving reached its artistic peak: carved Shoushan seals and ink stands became very popular during this period. A piece is always of course carved from a single stone, but there will probably be colour variations on that stone.

Fuzhou wood carving is another traditional craft. Obviously not so many pieces have been handed down, though some religious figures from the Song and Tang Dynasties can be seen. In Fuzhou *longyan* (Dragon-Eye) — of which there is a plentiful supply — and box, are the most popular woods. Old tree roots are also used for wooden sculpture, but one of the joys of *longyan* wood is its gnarled and twisting habit so that it indeed looks like a root, the finished product being a mixture of natural and man-made art.

Fujian ivory carving by comparison has a very short history. In the 1950s, when the supply of boxwood was becoming scarce, the government imported large amounts of Indian and African ivory and many boxwood sculptors duly transferred their skill to ivory. The majority of the pieces are of religious or historical figures. The work produced in the Fuzhou Carving Arts and Crafts Factory, which has won many prizes in national competitions, is of a generally high quality. Upstairs there is an area where pieces from the three crafts mentioned as well as sea-shell carving are on show and, of course, for sale.

A far older craft is lacquerware. Funereal objects made of lacquer have been unearthed from Han-Dynasty (206 BC–AD 220) tombs still intact. The type of lacquerware crafted in Fuzhou is called 'Bodiless lacquer' (*tuo tai*), and examples of this can be seen at the **Bodiless Lacquerware Factories**, the **Number One** on Wuyi Lu, the **Number Two** at Linjiang Lu. Unlike the Burmese or Japanese varieties which have bamboo or wooden frames, Fuzhou lacquer is cast. First a mould is formed (nowadays out of plastic) into which the liquid lacquer (sap from the lac tree) is poured. A month passes whilst it dries, then the mould is broken open and the piece polished and decorated.

The craft of cork pictures is relatively new. The story goes that around the turn of the century the then governor of Fujian, Xu Xijing, returned from a trip to Germany with a carved picture made of cork. He gave it to one Chen Chunren, a sculptor at the Institute of Arts and Crafts, and so cork pictures came to be included in the portfolio of Fuzhou crafts. The pictures are both flat or three-dimensional; the latter tend to be landscapes. Each little piece of the picture, whether a tree or petals of a flower, is carved separately, then pinned onto the picture and finally glued. The intricacy of the work is amazing and though each finished product may not be to everyone's taste, the craftsmen's work is a marvel of dexterity and concentration. The **Fuzhou Cork Carving Factory** is located in Wusi Lu.

The making of ox horn combs is an ancient craft with a traceable history of some 700 years, and is still carried on at the **Fuzhou Horn Comb Factory**, at Wenrufang. Many of the combs are in the shape of animals — perhaps a panda or a fish — with the face and body of the animal painted on. Sometimes the combs are made of sheep horn. They make excellent presents.

A visit to the **Fuzhou Umbrella Factory** at Yangzhong Lu is a delight. First one enters the room where the frames are made. The bamboo base has string plaited through it to achieve a cohesive shape. The next section is where the paper or silk is applied in strips and glued into place. The paper is then varnished with persimmón or tung oil and hung up to dry. Later they are decorated with traditional patterns. The umbrellas come in all shapes (some square) and sizes, colours and designs.

Shopping in Fuzhou

Shops of interest are dotted all over Fuzhou and as always it is fun and productive to choose an area and wander around: one can discover all sorts of little alleys and fascinating Aladdin's caves.

There are three main areas in which to wander: Wusi Lu (May 4th Road) near the Minjiang Hotel, Bayiqi Lu (August 17th Road) and

Taijiang Lu. Turn right out of the Minjiang and just past the entrance to the Overseas Chinese Hotel is a complex of arts and crafts shops. Each little section is run by a different group such as the Fuzhou Calligraphy and Painting Society. A rich miscellany of antiques, paintings, books, wood-carvings, traditional furniture, and even water heaters and fold-up beds are to be found here. At street level is a flower and bird shop, every inch of which is hung with bamboo bird cages, some with occupants. Others awaiting buyers are housed in rectangular mesh cages, with green leaves atop to protect them from the sun. One side of the shop is banked with potted miniature landscapes (*bonsai*) and an interesting selection of *nanmu* roots, polished, varnished and each with a flat top carved to house a potted plant. Just past this complex, turn right into Qingcheng Jie, the home of a food and vegetable market. This is a wide street (open only to pedestrians and bicyclists), lined with huge jacaranda trees; during the month of June it is carpeted with pale mauve blossom. At the Wusi Lu end are the fish and cooked-food stalls, and further along one comes to vegetable, fruit and flower stalls, all presented with artistry. Half-way down the street on the right (just opposite the herbal medicine stall) is an entrance guarded by two stone lions. This is the **Memorial Hall of Wang Shenzhi**, the Min King who was a sponsor of the temple on Drum Mountain (see page 38). It is a fairly plain but elegant courtyard house built in the Tang Dynasty and worth a quick look in if open. Continue on along Qingcheng Jie, through an archway, and proceed until you reach a crossroads. A wander along the street to right or left is worthwhile — for a mixture of shop houses and plain dwellings. Since many of the homes are so small, children do their homework at little tables in the street. Grannies sit at their front doors knitting whilst keeping an eye on their young charges.

The roundabout at Bayiqi Lu and Dongda Lu marks the centre of Fuzhou's shopping district in the downtown area. The **Dongjiekou Department Store** is on one side of this roundabout. It has nice fabrics, including batik from Yunnan, but otherwise nothing out of the ordinary. Wander along Bayiqi Lu to the **Friendship Store**. On the opposite side of the road is a **Foreign Languages Bookstore**. All the way down this street beside the main square (Wuyi Guangchang) is the **Fuzhou Antique Store.**

The third area is around the **Taijiang Department Store** at 117 Taijiang Lu. This is a very popular store, and in the surrounding streets there is a clothes market with an occasional fruit stall. During May succulent red bayberries (*Myrica rubra*), just the thing to quench the thirst of a shopper, are sold everywhere. Near here on the banks of a canal is a new shopping complex housed in an old-style building. The

shops downstairs are set up like an antique market, while a restaurant upstairs serves a range of snacks, now very well known in the West by their Cantonese name '*dim sum*'. A street not to be missed in this neighbourhood is the **Little Bridge Flower and Bird Market**. Stalls are hung with bamboo bird-cages of every conceivable design, most equipped with a porcelain drinking bowl and seed dish. Amongst the packets of seeds sit pot plants and *bonsai*. The *bonsai* enthusiast, however, should visit the **Fuzhou Flower and Potted Landscape Company** at theWuyi Lu and Wusi Lu roundabout near the Hitachi Fujian factory.

Sights in Fuzhou

Drum Mountain (Gu Shan)

Set amongst the beautiful scenery of Drum Mountain is the Gushing Spring Temple (Yongquan Si). Leave the city via the eastern suburbs, and in about 15 minutes you will arrive at the bottom of the mountain. There is a road that goes all the way to the top, but traditionally visitors climb up over 2,000 steps to reach the temple. For those feeling energetic and with time in hand, the steps begin just after the roundabout where the road to the temple starts to climb. The route is three and a half kilometres (two miles) long, twists and turns up the tree-covered mountain (crossing the road every now and then) and goes through eight pavilions. There is an interesting legend attached to the stairway. In ancient times the Gushing Stream Temple and the Xichan Temple (see page 46) were the two largest and most powerful temples in Fuzhou. The Abbot of Xichan was jealous of his fellow abbot's power and set about to destroy it. He suggested to his unsuspecting colleague that it was essential to build a stone stairway from the foot of the mountains to the Gushing Spring Temple to give pilgrims easy access. The stairway was finished and immediately the temple fell into disuse. Eventually the Abbot of Gushing Spring Temple understood: the stone stairway symbolized a venomous reptile slithering up the mountain to poison the temple. He immediately ordered eight pavilions to be built over the steps, thus dissecting the reptile into eight pieces. And a stone tablet bearing the name of Buddha was erected at the reptile's throat, thus delivering the death blow. Thereafter the temple prospered.

The route by road is equally picturesque, zigzagging up the mountain. Wild flowers bloom year-round, but especially lovely to see are azaleas, swags of white climbing roses and wild lilies which flower between the pines during April and May. Every now and then through a gap in the trees one catches a glimpse of the Min River far below.

Gushing Stream Temple (Yongquan Si) The approach to the temple complex is along a winding stone path edged with a high, deep red wall topped with tiles. An imposing gate with the traditional hipped roof marks the actual entrance. Go through the gate and turn right immediately through a moon gate in the wall. You will then be confronted by an imposing two-storey building which was the emperor's resting place (Weilong Ge). On each side of this building, now used as a shop, is a pond full of large healthy carp. Fine trees surround the water. Follow the path to the left of the pond and the Gushing Stream Temple comes into view.

The setting of this temple is magical. It is surrounded by mature trees, their leaves brilliant red and green against the backdrop of darker green tree-clad mountains. From here Drum Mountain itself lies to the right of the temple. (Today the Chinese Airforce have an early warning station up there.) Before the entrance steps there is a small hot spring well to throw a coin in for good fortune.

On either side of the temple stand two small, delicate porcelain pagodas of considerable artistic merit. These octagonal nine-storey pagodas were moulded in 1082 (the oldest known in Fujian). Each little roof has upturned eaves with bells hanging down from them. The walls are decorated with 1,038 statues of Buddha.

Next one enters the Hall of Kings. A statue of the fat jolly Maitreya Buddha sits in the middle of the hall welcoming visitors. One then passes into the main courtyard — a wonderful, totally enclosed space. Ahead, across a narrow stretch of water, is the Main Hall (Buddha's Holy Hall). Immediately to the left and right are the Bell and Drum Towers. These charming, two-storey towers have exaggerated hipped eaves, pale pink brickwork faced with a white diamond pattern, and they are crowned by stone pagodas. Late afternoon, when the sun's glow illuminates the pinks against the dark green of the woods behind, is a perfect time to visit.

From the top of either tower (a gentle climb up one flight of wooden steps) the view over the roofs is lovely.

Because it is still an active religious institution with 300 monks, the temple is a pleasure to visit. Services are held daily at 5 am and at 4 and 5 pm. Inside the Main Hall are three vast statues of Buddha, each sitting on a lotus, with 18 *arhats* (saints) on guard on either side. The painted ceiling dates from the Qing Dynasty. Above the wooden altar table hangs a continuously burning oil lamp. The air is thick with joss stick smoke and the smell of sandalwood (the powder is put in the incense burners). And on the stone floor row upon row of cassocks await the monks. During religious services, the monks chant to the beat of a drum, interrupted by the occasional high pitched ring of a bell. In the candlelit hall, with the heady atmosphere of incense, intoning monks, their elegant brown linen capes held in place by exquisite jade and amber clasps, and the three Buddha images gazing down, one feels transported to another world and another time. Several of the courtyards to the left of the Main Hall are at present under restoration. However, it is possible to see the three 800-year-old palms (*Cycas revoluta*), strange stubby trees set in a charming courtyard with porcelain inlay along the walls.

Take the stairway down the left side of the Main Hall and on the left you come to the kitchens. Some of the original cooking ware is still in use. There are four giant pans (*wok*), cast in 1034, capable of cooking rice for 1,000 people. The largest, with a diameter of 6.9 metres (156 feet), can hold a ton of water. The *woks* sit on brick stoves which are fuelled from behind. Watching the stoker at work, it looked as if he could well be a fireman on a steam train. It takes roughly an hour to bring the big *wok* full of water to the boil.

Continue down the steps on the left and, in the far left hand corner of the courtyard, is a door which leads to the library. This hall was built in 1660 and contains 9,000 volumes of the Tripitaka; 657 of these date from the Qing Dynasty and are illuminated with blood and silver. The oldest copies date from the Ming Dynasty. The librarian speaks good English and is eager to talk about the treasures under his care. Also of interest here is a small white jade reclining Buddha, shown about to enter Nirvana.

Linyuan Cave To visit the cave, which is part of the complex, go out through the Hall of Kings, down the steps past the porcelain pagodas. Turn left through an orchard of magnolias, walk around the pond in front of the emperor's resting place where, in the left hand corner, is a path leading to the cave. It is in fact more a ravine than a cave, entered by a steep flight of stairs. The rocks above are covered with characters, the largest of which — the familiar 'longevity' character — was carved by the Song-Dynasty scholar Zhu Xi. Follow the path to a teahouse built against the cliff, where the monks serve tea made with spring water. Both this teahouse and the souvenir shop shut just before 4 pm when the monks go to attend their evening service.

Yu Hill (Yu Shan)

Of the three hills which straddle Fuzhou, Yu Hill is the most interesting to visit. The hill is some 60 metres (196 feet) above sea level and covers around 6.5 hectares (16 acres).

A suggested route around the sights on the hill is as follows. Start climbing the hill by the entrance to the Yushan Hotel. At the top of the incline, at the entrance to the Yu Hill, stands the **Nine Immortals Cave** (Jiuxian Dong) and well. Nine brothers of the He family who lived during the Han Dynasty (260 BC–AD 220) were expelled by their father, who was angered by the fact that eight of his sons were blind and one partially so. The father's plan to poison his sons was overheard by the partially blind one who then led his brothers to this cave. Here they lived to a very great age and made their immortal pills in the adjacent well. When they eventually died and became the Nine Immortals, they rose to the skies as carp. Just past the well there are steps leading up to the left. At the top is a large platform shaded by an aged banyan tree. Every day around 3 pm a musical gathering is held here, organized by one of the retirement associations. Amateurs and semi-professionals come and try their luck.

Just above the musical stage is the **Goddess of Mercy Temple** (Guanyin Si). The original hall was built in the Tang Dynasty although the present building dates from Emperor Kangxi's time (1662–1721). The main hall will soon house the Fuzhou City Museum.

Leaving the temple, continue around the hill anti-clockwise, past the vast Lion Rock on the left. When the path joins the main one, turn right and it will lead to the **Nine Immortals Temple** (Jiuxian Guan). This was originally a Daoist (Taoist) temple built around 1087. The building was destroyed by fire in 1922, but it was immediately rebuilt. The layout is quite different from that of most temple complexes: the entrance is at the side; ahead are two main halls facing each other and joined by a pavilion with an extremely complicated inner roof. This would have been the bell tower. These halls were intended for the worship of the Jade Emperor and the Nine Immortals of the He family. The carved stone pillars outside are an example of the exquisite work by the Hui'an people (see page 81). Today the halls house the exhibits of the Yu Hill Society of Painting and Calligraphy. It is worth climbing up the rickety stairs in the left-hand hall to the first-floor balcony where one gets a fine view of the city below.

To reach the **Drunken Rock** (Zuishi) and **Memorial Hall to General Qi Jiguang** (1528–87), one must go back along the main path past the Nine Immortals Well where there is a discreet door in a wall. Outside there is often a hawker or two selling sweet or savoury olives on sticks (a great Fuzhou delicacy). Immediately beyond the door is a covered walkway with a collection of old photographs of Fuzhou sights mounted on the wall. The walkway leads up to the Drunken Rock and a memorial hall which was used by an American church. The story of General Qi Jiguang has a sad twist. Towards the end of the Ming

Dynasty the general was engaged in fighting Japanese pirates. After one of his battles he beheaded his son for retreating in the face of the enemy. When he was finally victorious the general came to Yu Hill to celebrate. He got drunk and lay down on the bed-shaped rock, which then became known as Drunken Rock. On it is carved a poem written by Yu Dafu in 1936. It praises the general for making the pirates tremble with fear and offers condolences for the loss of his son. Behind the rock is a small pavilion which General Qi built in memory of his son. Further uphill is the Memorial Hall to General Qi.

Just below the Memorial Hall is a small museum. At present the exhibition is of a dig to exhume the corpse of a well-to-do lady. The clothes in which she was buried are on show, perfectly intact. and so is she! The corpse lies in a yellow liquid; the intestines have been removed so there is a lot of stitch-work up her front. The skin is a little leathery looking — the effect of coming into contact with air when the body was unwrapped. Also on show is a very interesting photographic record of the dig itself. Although it may sound gruesome, the exhibition is a fascinating record of early Ming times.

Below is the **White Pagoda** (Bai Ta) which — along with the Ebony Pagoda to the west on Wu Shan — is visible from all over Fuzhou. It is an octagonal seven-storey building made of brick and wood, and then gilded. It was erected in 904 by the King of Min in gratitude to his parents. In 1534, it was struck by lightning and its outer wooden skin charred. By 1548 it had been rebuilt; this time its exterior was plastered and painted white. Just north of the White Pagoda is the **White Pagoda Temple** which dates originally from 905. Today the temple is used as a library. The carving on the stone pillars inside and out is magnificent, again the work of Hui'an craftsmen.

Wu Shan (Black Hill or Crow Hill)

Wu Shan lies directly west of Yu Hill, is some 60 metres (196 feet) high and covers an area of 17 hectares (42 acres). The hill was once famous for its Daoist temples and shrines, but today the only relic on the hill of any note is the Ebony Pagoda.

Ebony Pagoda (Wu Pagoda) The Ebony Pagoda dates from 799, when it was built in celebration of the reigning Tang emperor's birthday. This octagonal pagoda is seven storeys high — not nine as originally planned — and built of stone decorated with niches and small doors. Time and uprisings have dealt unkindly with the Ebony Pagoda; many of the little Buddhas in the niches are defaced or removed, and it has a general feeling of abandonment.

On the west side of the hill overlooking the pagoda stands a small courtyard temple to the Jade Emperor. According to tradition, Lao Zi, one of the founders of Daoism, is also patron of this temple.

Screen Mountain (Ping Shan)

Fuzhou's third mountain, or rather hill, lies to the north of the city and is so called as it protects the city from the ravages of the north (the direction from which all bad things are thought to come in China) and also, of course, served as a watchtower. Like those at Wu Shan, Ping Shan's monuments have fallen foul either to the passage of time or war. Of its 29 historical sights only the **Hualin Temple** remains of any interest. The main hall is a wooden construction dating from 963 and as such is one of the oldest in southern China. Although not really worthy of a special visit, it can be conveniently combined with the Chongfu Temple (see page 49), itself worth a visit.

Lin Zexu Memorial Hall

In the middle of a residential street west of Nanhou Jie one comes upon an unassuming gate in a white-washed wall. It is the entrance to the Lin Zexu Memorial Hall. Lin was born in Fuzhou in 1785. By all accounts Lin was a sensitive man, ahead of his time, especially in his regard for those less well off than himself. In his early career he served in Fujian as a magistrate and as Prefect of Justice and of Finance. Later he became governor and imperial envoy in both Jiangsu and Zhejiang Provinces.

Lin Zexu became world famous for his part in the anti-opium movement. In 1839 he was appointed Special Imperial Envoy in Canton to deal with the opium question. By this time the 'foreign devils' (European and American merchants) were profiting substantially from the illicit opium trade; in 1837 a mere 230 foreign merchants lived in Canton and that year 40,000 chests of opium were sold. Within a week of his arrival in Canton Commissioner Lin blockaded the 'factories' (warehouses). He told the merchants that if they surrendered the opium he would lift the blockade. To his surprise, 20,000 chests were handed over and ceremoniously burnt by the Commissioner. However, opium traffic continued, albeit not as overtly as before. When some British and American sailors accidentally killed a local villager, Commissioner Lin demanded that the guilty man be handed over for trial. When this was refused he blockaded the factories yet again. This time the 'foreign devils' retreated to Hong Kong waters whence they continued to trade. A furious Commissioner

Lin ordered his war junks to intercept food supplies being ferried by local tradesmen. But the commissioner had not reckoned with the British Navy which opened fire and sank four of his war junks. So began the first Opium War. Commissioner Lin became the scapegoat of the war, and was exiled to Xinjiang Province in the northwest of China. While there he became ill and so was allowed to move to Xi'an. However, in 1845, he was reinstated, taking up first the Governorship of Shaanxi and Gansu, and later of Yunnan. His success in these posts led to his being given the title of 'Teacher of the Prince', second only in prestige to that of Prime Minister. In September 1850, Lin was appointed the Special Imperial Envoy to suppress the Taiping uprising (in and around Nanjing), but he died at the age of 65 on his way to take up his post.

The memorial hall is a traditional courtyard house. One enters off the street into a little courtyard. There follows a ceremonial entrance arch and a long strip of garden, with whispering bamboo on either side of a path that leads to three steles. On these tablets are engraved a funeral oration written by the emperor, an imperial edict pardoning Commissioner Lin and a funeral record. The path then leads right into a hall. Here sits a statue of Commissioner Lin looking serious and scholarly (he was an excellent calligrapher). On the walls is a fascinating collection of contemporary photographs and water-colours accompanied by a commentary (in Chinese only) on Lin's life and work. The exhibition continues through the rest of the house. The garden which surrounds the house and, in the traditional way, becomes part of it, is a charming creation of water, stones and architectural shapes; it is the quintessence of a Chinese garden.

West Lake and Park

This lake was dug in AD 282, the excavated material being used to build a city wall, while the water irrigated the fields. It was during the Five Dynasties period (907−60) that Wang Shenzhi styled himself the King of Min as well as Emperor. He turned the lake into an imperial garden. A temporary palace, called the Crystal Palace, was built in the centre of the lake, from which, the local chronicles suggest, the king would sail around the lake on a pleasure boat tended by beautiful maidens. During the Song Dynasty the lake was widened and enlarged to its present size. Under the sponsorship of Commissioner Lin Zexu the lake was dredged and edged with stone. The West Lake was opened as a park in 1949.

Kaihua Temple Kaihua Temple on the mid-lake island is now used as an exhibition hall — in the autumn for an annual chrysanthemum

show, in the spring for a narcissus one, and so on. A temple was first built on this site during the Tang Dynasty (618−907), and later the King of Min's Crystal Palace stood here. The present Kaihua Temple was built in 1705.

Zoo At the southwestern corner of the West Lake Park is the Fuzhou Zoo. It is a nice clean zoo, and all the animals look well cared for in a pleasing environment surrounded by parkland. As well as many commonly kept animals, there are four giant pandas here.

Fujian Provincial Museum

On the western edge of the park is the Fujian Provincial Museum (open daily 8.30 am−4 pm). It is filled with interesting exhibits; however, at the time of writing there were no English captions to the displays. Perhaps the most interesting exhibit is a coffin from Wuyi Mountain. Made of a trunk of *nanmu* (a hardwood), it has been dated at 3,445 years old. Inside is a skeleton lying on a bamboo mat, with some funeral offerings by the side. The astonishing aspect of this exhibit is that it was found 51 metres (167 feet) up a cliff face in Wuyi Mountain. Anthropologists and archaeologists are still unable to decide why these people buried their dead in caves way up a sheer rock-face above a fast flowing river and, indeed, how they got them up there. There is a photographic record of the coffin being removed in 1978 — obviously a fearsome task. Another interesting exhibit is of Song-Dynasty bricks decorated with a fish-bone pattern. Today, all over Fujian, though especially around the Quanzhou area, patterned bricks are seen, in old and new buildings alike. A red brick wall might have a black diamond pattern or a feather brush-stroke effect. Two embalmed bodies, a man and his wife, surprise one on entering a small room towards the end of the museum tour. They were embalmed around 1558 and are perfectly preserved. They now look a little leathery but easier on the eye than the lady in Yu Shan (see page 41), as they are not displayed in yellow liquid, though the bottles containing the intestines are close by.

Xichan Temple

Due west of the city, just past Fuzhou University, is Xichan Temple. The temple dates from 867, but since then it has been restored and renovated many times. Today yet more renovation and building is in progress — the result of generous donations from overseas Chinese, mainly from Singapore.

One now enters at the side of the Main Hall; unfortunately, one misses the first impact of the pleasing building by this route. Two brightly coloured three-storey pagodas have recently been placed on either side of the Main Hall. When asked to comment on these new additions, one of the monks shrugged his shoulders, implying that if believers were generous enough to donate such things, how could the inmates object? Inside, the hall encompasses a magnificent space; the roof high-vaulted, the ceiling divided into squares painted with dragons, pheasants and other birds and animals, from which long wooden banners (*fan*) hang down. The three vast Buddhas have recently been re-coated in 200 kilograms (441 pounds) of gold and then, unfortunately, rather badly lacquered.

Behind the hall, across a garden, is the Hall of Prayer. In the garden between the two halls grows a lychee tree some 800 years old which still bears fruit. After the grand, somewhat impersonal Main Hall, this prayer hall is small, intimate and, as yet, not over-restored. Up the pillars climb dragons carved by Hui'an craftsmen, 24 heavenly kings line the walls, and an old gold cloth covers the altar decorated with vases of fresh flowers. The Scripture Hall, part of the Qing-Dynasty extensions, stands behind the Hall of Prayer. Recently the Jade Buddha Hall has been finished, built with money donated by Burmese Chinese, and it houses two jade Buddhas carved in Mandalay. There is an interesting view of the roofscape of the temple complex from the first floor of the Jade Buddha Hall.

Today 130 monks, many of them novices, are in residence here. The more senior monks live in rooms alongside the Hall of Prayer; new quarters as well as a restaurant and rooms for visitors have been built beside the Jade Buddha Hall. Visitors anxious not to be jostled by crowds should avoid visiting this popular temple on Sundays or public holidays.

Sights outside Fuzhou

Gold Mountain Temple (Jinshan Temple)

The Gold Mountain Temple, otherwise a nice but ordinary building, is transformed by its dramatic position into a truly stunning place to visit. It sits perched on a reef in the middle of the Wulong Jiang (Black Dragon River). The story goes that during the Song Dynasty the area around Fuzhou suffered a drought. On this reef was a well, which, like the majority in the area, had run dry. A certain lady, who had once drunk from the well and had since become a holy person, returned to pray for water. Sure enough, water sprang from the rock. From then

on, the local people were able to benefit from the constantly filled
well, and to show their gratitude, they built a temple. A stone pagoda
seven storeys high was erected over the actual crack in the rocks where
water sprang. When one looks at the temple from the shore, the
pagoda can be seen rising from the middle of the building.

Visitors are poled across the water to the temple in a small canoe-
type craft. There are two halls on the reef, the main one (on the
upstream side) is dedicated to the Goddess of Mercy. From this small
dark room the view is directly upriver. Groups of little fishing boats
with square sails glide along the water, endlessly being poled upstream
past the temple and then slipping back again. At the rear of the temple
(downstream end) is an empty room which is now used for picnicking
visitors. (On holidays the temple and its adjoining sand bar — when
the water is not too high — are packed.) Between the two halls is an
open space with a white stone pagoda perched on the rock. It is said
that the temple has the shape of an emperor's seal floating in the
water. Today, this building is the home of two monks and two nuns.

The one drawback to visiting the Gold Mountain Temple is that
very few people in Fuzhou seem to know where it is. In fact, getting
there is very simple. Take Dongda Lu out of the city, crossing the Min
River by the Hengshan Bridge, and keep straight on until the road
reaches the village of Hongtang. Wind through the village until the
road comes to a T-junction (the river forming the top of the T), turn
right along the river and, after a bumpy ten minutes or so, the temple
comes into view on the left. At present it is well worth the effort.
However, there are plans to construct a large bridge across the Wulong
River just above the temple; it is hard to imagine what that would do
to the tranquil feeling of the place.

Chongfu Temple

This nunnery, once a monastery, north of the Fuzhou railway station, was very badly damaged during the Cultural Revolution. Although it has now been totally repaired, it is nonetheless somewhat lacking in atmosphere. It was originally built during the Tang Dynasty. An interesting feature of this monastery is its close relationship with a monastery of the same name at Nagasaki in Japan. From 1629 and for 11 generations, the abbots of the Japanese monastery came from its sister establishment in Fuzhou; indeed the monastery in Nagasaki is popularly known as the Fuzhou Monastery. In 1957, it became a nunnery and today it is also the home of the Buddhist school of Fuzhou. About half of the 150 nuns in residence are students. One section of the monastery is set aside as an old people's home.

The nuns also run a crematorium here and, a little way up the hill at the back of the monastery, stand a dagoba, a pagoda, and a funeral hall. The bodies are encased in a sitting position in special wooden coffins before cremation. The ashes are then collected and stored in porcelain jars in the funeral hall. From then on the relatives come here to pay their respects. The land which surrounds the temple complex is farmed by the nuns; they grow tea, and also make their own incense.

Snow Peak Temple (Xuefeng Si)

The drive north from Fuzhou to Snow Peak Temple is through quintessential Chinese countryside, spread with terraced paddy fields, the vibrant green of the nursery sections glowing amongst the more mature squares of rice. You can see bending figures transplanting the young rice, old people or children tending flocks of ducks, clumps of trees which shade small villages, and the whole surrounded by hills. Snow Peak is some 77 kilometres (48 miles) from the city. The story is that in 870 a monk called Yicun received an inspiration that the mountain would be an auspicious site to build a temple. One day he climbed to the summit and was forced to spend the night there due to a snowstorm. Later, on being asked by the King of Min to describe the peak, Yicun answered that even in summer it was snow clad; thereafter it was named Snow Peak.

There are in fact two temples to visit at this site: the **Temple of the Worship of the Saints** (Chongsheng Si) and, a few minutes' walk away, the small **Withered Wood Temple** (Gumu An). At present the main temple is undergoing extensive renovation, thanks to donations by Singaporean Chinese. In front of the entrance hall stand four magnificent tamarisk trees; two are thought to have been planted by the Abbot Yicun, two by the King of Min. The entrance hall has bright red walls and pillars, a dark green tiled roof, with a double roofed porch (blue tiles separating the two roofs). It is the most pleasing building of the complex, especially with the magnificent trees in the forecourt. At the far end of a stone courtyard bisected by water is the Main Hall; inside are three jade statues of the Buddha. And to the right of the Doctrine Hall is a bell-shaped pagoda of stone which is said to hold the ashes of Abbot Yicun.

Eighty monks live in the monastery today. In addition to performing religious duties, they run a successful agricultural enterprise. From their three hectares (about eight acres) of land they grow, amongst other produce, some 10,000 kilograms (10 tons) of rice and 30,000 kilograms (30 tons) of potatoes a year as well as their own brand of 'Snow Peak' tea.

Across the road, a few minutes' walk along a path amongst the fields, is the enchanting Withered Wood Temple. This is a small, pink building with one room on the ground floor, an outhouse on either side, and a tiny upper room, hence the upper roof. It is really a 'face' house: the central door has a double-sided gate which folds back onto the wall, forming the nose and smiling mouth, and the two round window on either side of the door represent the eyes. The double roof gives the 'face' a complicated coiffure. The path leads around the pond, giving the visitor plenty of time to absorb the temple's charm. The Withered Wood Temple was also built around 870. Inside the temple is the knarled trunk of a tree, thought to be over a thousand years old. Inside and out the hollow trunk is covered with inscriptions mostly from the Song and Ming Dynasties, which the passage of time has rendered indistinct. The species of the tree has never been decided. For the past ten years one solitary monk has lived here.

Mawei Port

Mawei (meaning literally Horse's Tail) is the port of Fuzhou city, but is itself nine kilometres (5.6 miles) from the sea. A port has existed there for centuries: shipbuilding is recorded as early as the Spring and Autumn period (770–256 BC). Several sailing junks for the renowned Ming admiral, Zheng He, were constructed at Mawei. Its importance increased in 1842 when, after the signing of the Treaty of Nanking, Fuzhou became a Treaty Port. In fact, many of the European merchants preferred Mawei to Fuzhou itself, their legacy surviving today in the form of the European-style houses to be found in many of its narrow streets.

Today the commercial port has been greatly enlarged and now has the capacity to handle large ocean-going vessels. In 1984 an area near the port was designated as an economic and development zone. Some 3,000 people are employed in the shipbuilding industry. There is also still a large naval base here which explains why half the town is out of bounds for foreigners. A trip to Mawei takes at least half a day.

Luoxing Pagoda

Out on a spit of land overlooking the entrance to the harbour stands the Luoxing Pagoda, which was first built in the Song Dynasty. There are many legends attached to this pagoda all involving abandoned ladies. The most famous one concerns the wife of a seaman who would come every day to watch for her husband's ship to return, but always in vain. Eventually she collected enough money to build the pagoda which she hoped would act as a beacon. One day her husband did indeed sail up the estuary but, seeing the pagoda, he thought he had missed his way and so sailed off.

Set in a little park, the Luoxing is an octagonal stone construction of seven storeys. A bell hangs from each corner of the upturned eaves — so on a windy day there is a constant tinkle.

Maritime Memorial Hall

This memorial hall is dedicated to all those who lost their lives during both Opium Wars against the British and during the Sino-French battles in the Mawei estuary. The exhibits inside include biographies of Shen and Zuo, credited with founding China's modern 19th-century navy (the former was a son-in-law of Commissioner Lin of Opium War fame). They organized exhanges of naval students with France and had battle ships (equipped with Krupp guns) built in Germany — an international approach in marked contrast to China's prevailing mood of the time. There are also paintings and maps of the final stages of the Mawei Sea Battle in 1884 including a 'rogues gallery' of the French officers. It was as a result of this battle and the subsequent Treaty of Tientsin that France gained control of the Chinese tributary state of Vietnam (but at the same time gave up control of Taiwan and the Pescadores). The building which houses this memorial hall is a courtyard-style house; beside it is a mass grave of the men killed during the sea battle. On the hill behind the house stand a fortress and some cannons. Other memorabilia include cannon balls, clothing of the Chinese admirals, a charming Yixing tea set presumably used on the admiral's ship.

Wuyi Mountain

The Wuyi Shan area is a beautiful mountain resort on the southern border of the county of Chong'an, northwest of Fuzhou. The designated Wuyi resort area is roughly 60 square kilometres (23 square miles). The best time to visit is during the autumn months when the skies are clear and the Nine-twist Stream is sparkling. From March to May or June the area is reminiscent of the Chinese mountainscapes loved by traditional artists.

Wuyi has been a favourite mountain retreat of Chinese literati over the centuries. As far back as the Qin (221−207 BC) and Han (206 BC−AD 220) Dynasties it is known to have been visited by poets and painters — particularly remarkable in view of the arduous journey in those days. Emperor Wudi of the Han Dynasty (reigned 140−87 BC) sent his courtiers to build an altar just north of the Nine-twist Stream on which to place offerings to the Lord of Wuyi. Later the altar was incorporated into a palace, a building which survives today.

As well as a documented history of Wuyi, there is a wealth of legendary history. Some 5,000 years ago, during the reign of Emperor Yao, a wise old man named Peng Zu (who lived for 700 years!) made his home in Wuyi. The Jian River was then a rushing torrent which constantly flooded the surrounding area. The old man instructed his two sons Peng Wu and Peng Yi to cut through the mountain and thus to create the tributary, Nine-twist Stream, at the same time excavating the surrounding land for farming. Hence the area was named 'Wuyi', incorporating the two sons' names. There is an alternative, if less colourful, explanation of the name: the first character translates as 'militant' (*Wu*), and Yi is the collective name for the minority tribes of southeast China, and thus the words combine to represent the area inhabited by the militant Yi tribe.

Many of the stories centre on the Lord of Wuyi, a semi-legendary character (comparable to England's King Arthur) of Han-Dynasty times. One legend about Lord Wuyi describes him as being sent by the Jade Emperor of Heaven to settle in Wuyi to cultivate the land and grow (immortal) medicinal herbs with the help of the local Immortals. He held a banquet for 2,000 local people, who were transported to a beautiful palace by a rainbow bridge leading across the rocks to the peak. At the banquet's end they returned home by the rainbow bridge. No sooner had they reached the other end than a hurricane came up, breaking the bridge into fragments, which became the various crags, peaks and caves of Wuyi.

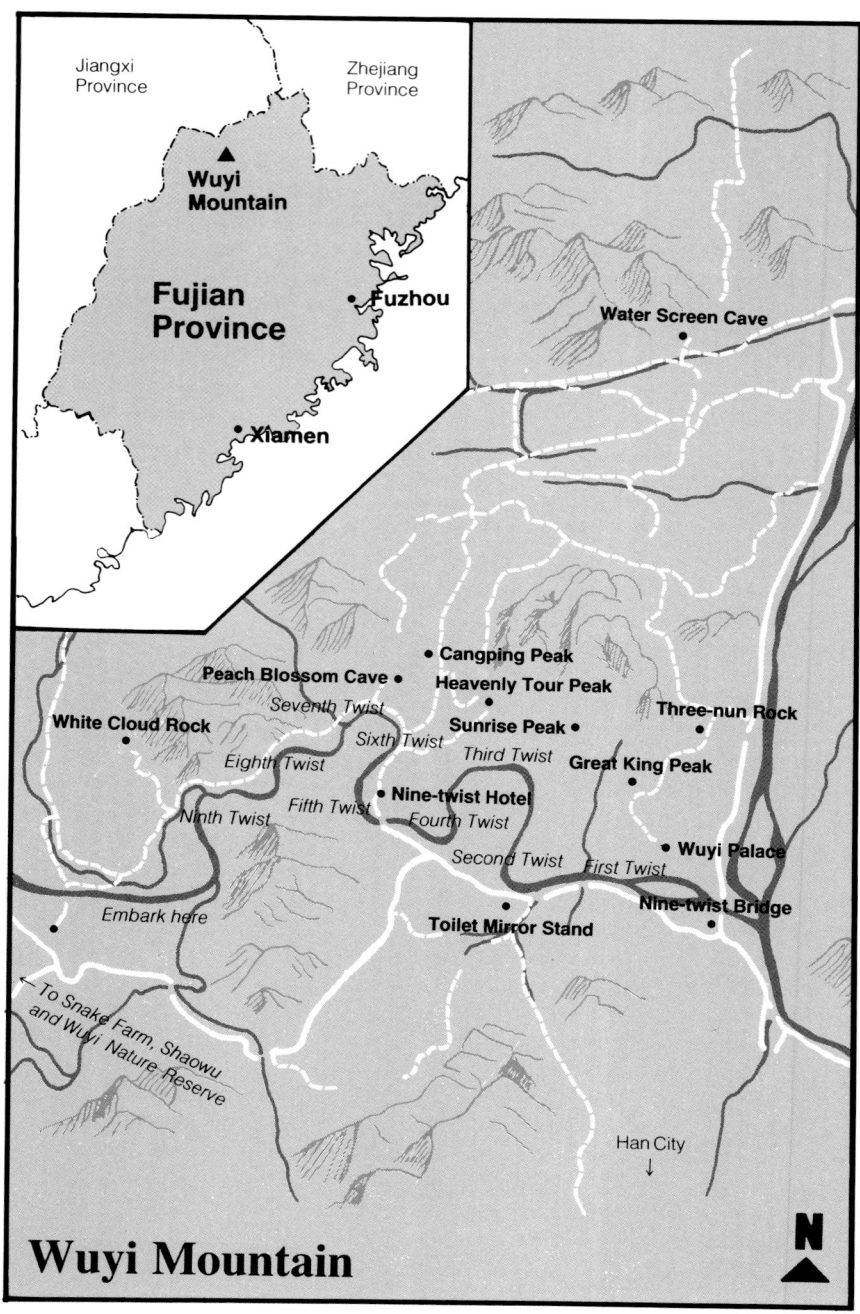

Jiangxi Province

Zhejiang Province

▲
Wuyi Mountain

Fujian Province

• **Fuzhou**

• **Xiamen**

Water Screen Cave

• Cangping Peak

Peach Blossom Cave • **Heavenly Tour Peak**

Seventh Twist

White Cloud Rock • **Sunrise Peak** • Three-nun Rock

Eighth Twist *Sixth Twist* *Third Twist*

Great King Peak

Fifth Twist • **Nine-twist Hotel**

Ninth Twist *Fourth Twist*

Second Twist *First Twist* • **Wuyi Palace**

Embark here **Nine-twist Bridge**

← To Snake Farm, Shaowu and Wuyi Nature Reserve **Toilet Mirror Stand**

Han City ↓

N ▲

Wuyi Mountain

There are direct buses to Wuyi from Fuzhou. To get to Wuyi from Fuzhou by train you can go only as far as Nanping from the southeast. Then, from Nanping, it is another five hours' ride by car to Wuyi.

It is also possible to take a 12-hour boat ride from Fuzhou to Nanping and then go by road.

Hotels in Wuyi

Wuyi Mountain Villa
Wuyi Mountain
Scenic Area,
Chong'an County

武夷山房
武夷风景区

32 double rooms, Rmb45; 2 suites, Rmb90

Opened by CTS in July 1984, this pleasant hotel beside the Nine-twist Stream commands an excellent view of the Wuyi peaks. The hotel is built in traditional Northern Min (courtyard) style, with galleries joining living and sleeping quarters. The Nanjing Engineering Centre and the Fujian Design Centre designed the interiors and furniture, the latter being mostly bamboo, good-looking in a chunky way, and certainly a relief from the usual hotel fittings.

Manting Villa
Wuyi Mountain
Scenic Area,
Chong'an County
tel. through county
telephone
switchboard

幔亭山房
武夷风景区

38 double rooms, Rmb50; suites, Rmb55

Opened in June 1983 and run by CITS, this hotel is a bit scruffier than the Wuyi Mountain Villa next door but of much the same design. All rooms have baths, and some have air-conditioning. The food is better than at the Wuyi Mountain Villa.

Wuyi Guesthouse
150 Zhong Jie,
Chong'an

武夷宾馆
崇安县中街150号

80 rooms with no air-conditioning. Restaurant, coffee shop, disco.

Although situated in the small town of Chong'an, some distance from the main sights of Wuyi, this old-style hotel has charm, and the town itself is not without interest. The food is delicious, though some visitors were once served — to their horror — a puma. After dinner they were shown the pelt.

Wuyi Tea

Tea has been grown around Wuyi for 1,000 years; it has been regarded as one of China's best teas and exported all over the world. England and Germany have been customers for some 400 years, and the Queen of England herself is reputed to enjoy the Wuyi brew. In fact, 200 years ago all tea imported into England was known as Wuyi Tea.

Some 2,000 varieties of tea are produced in Wuyi, but the bulk is of the Oolong variety — famous for its mild flavour and unique fragrance — and 500 tons are produced annually. Tea leaves come from an evergreen shrub called *Camellia sinensis*, of which there are many varieties. However, it is not the variety of bush which produces the different types of tea — say Oolong or Jasmine — it is the method of processing. Throughout the year the tea bush is pruned constantly to stimulate the growth of young shoots, and it is these new leaves which are picked.

The leaves are harvested three times a year. Those destined to become Oolong are brought to the factory and immediately put onto a series of conveyor belts where hot and cold air is blown over them to remove most of the moisture. Later, they are transferred onto rollers for ten to 12 hours. This breaks down their juices, causing the leaves to go red. Next they are cooked at 148°C (300°F) for six minutes to fix oxidation. At this point many of the leaves are still attached to twigs (now the only source of moisture). Next they are cut into strips, though the twigs are still not discarded. They go back onto a belt and into another oven, this time for 20 minutes before being cooled, and put through the process a second time. At this point the leaves could be used to make tea, though it would be of an inferior quality. The sorting process comes next. In several large rooms chattering women sit at low tables, each one with a bamboo chair placed on a flat basket to catch falling leaves. Here the leaves, some in flat panniers, others in vast baskets, are meticulously sorted into thick and thin, small and big, and at last removed from their twigs. The tea is sorted several times and then the good-quality ones are packaged for storage (the small leaves will produce the strong tea, the large ones the weak). The inferior-quality leaves will be sold cheaply at this stage. After six months the packets are opened, reprocessed, graded, tasted and repacked accordingly.

The medicinal properties of tea are taken very seriously. The Institute of Traditional Chinese Medicine and Pharmacology of Fujian Province has recently conducted research into the effects of tea drinking (they used Oolong) on general health. They concluded that frequent tea drinking helped to slow down ageing and was good for preventing and curing cardiac and cerebral vascular diseases and for many other ailments. Wuyi Black Dragon Tea is advertised as a cure for hangovers, high blood pressure, bad temper and as a tonic for making the drinker feel generally alert.

Picking the leaves of young tea shrubs

The Jardine Matheson tea clipper 'Falcon' that plied between Fuzhou and Europe

Sights in Wuyi

Nine-twist Stream (Jiuqu Xi)

Locally this stretch of stream is named 'three-three' and 'six-six', the former referring to the nine bends in the stream, the latter to the 36 peaks which rise on either side. A long bamboo raft is the mode of transport along the 7.5 kilometres (4.6 miles) of the Nine-twist Stream. Some 14 sturdy bamboo poles are lashed together, on top of which sit bamboo armchairs. Each raft is piloted by two men, one who stands on the upward sloping bow, one on the stern, with bamboo poles for manoeuvering.

There is a tea-room at the jetty where one gets onto the rafts. On a sunny day straw hats will be provided or, in the wet season, plastic raincoats. (It is also possible to make this trip at night in the moonlight). During the first ten minutes or so of the journey the stream flows at a sedate pace and is quite wide. The banks are a favourite haunt of water buffalo — sometimes only the upper humps of their bodies are visible, giving one quite a shock when a brown boulder turns into a buffalo. A mass of flowers grow along the banks, including wild gardenias and lilies in the early summer.

The Ninth Twist is actually the first bend in the stream. Where possible the rock formations are likened to animals, although it is sometimes hard to find the resemblance. Just by the first rapid two lions sit playing ball. Around each bend are several points of interest: at the Ninth Twist towers **White Cloud Rock**, one of the highest peaks along the stream. This impressive peak stands on the north side of the stream and is often shrouded in clouds. On it can be seen the remains of the **White Cloud Monastery** and, at the bottom of the peak on the far side, is the reading room of Lu Donglai, a Song-Dynasty philosopher.

At the Eighth Twist the **Water Tortoise Stones** lie by the water's edge. These are said to resemble a small tortoise creeping onto the back of a larger one, and are actually quite easy to identify. Of the other scenes the narrow, elegant stone named after the **Goddess of Mercy Rock** (Guanyin Shi) is the most striking. The **Three Peaks Facing Upwards** which stand by the Seventh Twist are likened by some to three monks, two old, one young. Around the Sixth Twist are two scenes which are well worth visiting on foot as a separate excursion — namely Peach Blossom Cave and Heavenly Tour Peak (see below). At the Fifth Twist, half-way downstream, the land on either side opens out and **Hidden Screen Rock** stands a little way from the water. The huge rock is pleated and its sheer sides topped with vegetation. At the foot of the screen is the **Luohan Rock** — a meditating monk, with bent, bald head.

It was on the level land at this Fifth Twist that the Exquisite Building of Wuyi was erected in 1183 by the Song-Dynasty philosopher Zhu Xi. It consisted of halls, pavilions and teahouses and was used as a sort of club by visiting literati. It was destroyed in 1365, but was rebuilt in 1448 by the descendants of Zhu Xi. Renamed **Wengong Memorial Hall** (the memorial hall of the reverend literary man), it was also refurbished and repaired in 1708 during the reign of the Qing emperor Kangxi. Today it is the Nine-twist Hotel.

Big Treasure Peak, the landmark at the Fourth Twist, consists of a gently rolling mountain on which lies the **Immense Rock**, the **Inaccessible Caverns** and the **Unfathomable Pool**. There is a legend for virtually every rock formation. This pool is said to be the home of a venomous dragon which would sometimes rush out of the pond followed by nine small dragons. They would chase each other, brandishing their claws and frightening the local people. A passing Immortal killed them one by one, until he came to the smallest and youngest dragon, who wagged his tail at the Immortal and begged to be spared. His wish was granted on the understanding of future good behaviour. The dragon kept his word and continues to hide in the deep pool, protecting the mountain.

The most interesting historical site along the stream is at the Third Twist. High up on the sheer rock face of the **Small Treasure Peak** which stands on the south bank are found small entrances; inside are several boat-shaped coffins which lie on the so-called **Rainbow Bridge Planks**. The coffins are thought to be about 3,800 years old and to belong to the mountain's original inhabitants, the Yi minority. They were a fishing people for whom a boat was a prized possession. So it was natural to honour their dead by laying them to rest in a boat. Legend of course creeps into this extraordinary story. The planks on which the boats lie are said to be fragments of the Rainbow Bridge in the Lord of Wuyi tale. Although it is impossible to visit these caves to see the coffins, one has been removed and is on view in the Fuzhou Museum. The last two explanations for the twists of the stream are also intertwined with fable. The **Jade Beauty Rock** stands on the south bank at the Second Twist — a tall, elegant rock crowned with grass and wild flowers and reminiscent of a maiden, her long hair coiled and dressed with ornaments, the rock face folding like a dress. In front of her is a bathing pool, to her right a rock named **Toilet Mirror Stand**. At the First Twist stands the **Great King Peak**. The story goes that a family of Immortals came to visit earth, and the youngest sister fell in love with a handsome tea planter. A ghost named Iron Plate reported

the attachment to the Jade Emperor, and was ordered to bring her back to heaven. When she refused she was turned into the Jade Beauty Rock and her earthly lover into the Great King Peak. The ghost placed himself between them and became the Iron Plate Rock, thus preventing them from seeing each other ever again. Someone, perhaps the Jade Emperor himself, apparently felt sorry for the Jade Beauty, for by her side was placed the Toilet Mirror Stand, so she can look back at her lover and he at her reflection in the water.

Also at the First Twist is Wuyi Palace (see page 62). It is near the Manting Villa, one of Wuyi's new hotels, and easy to visit on foot. Just past the Great King Peak is the quay where the two-hour journey ends (though not for the boatmen, who have to pole upstream again).

A meander down the Nine-twist Stream, surrounded by exquisite scenery, flowers and birds, a mix of history and legend, can provide an afternoon of pure magic.

Heavenly Tour Peak

At the summit of Heavenly Tour Peak is the **Sky Tour Pavilion** from which the view is stunning. The peak stands at the Sixth Twist, more or less at the mid station of the Nine-twist Stream. One gets a total view of the nine twists as well as the surrounding countryside. It is a good idea to take the raft trip before climbing this peak so that one can then identify the landmarks. Try and make the climb at either dawn or dusk when the light is especially magical. The view from the top of the peak at the beginning of June, the end of the rainy season, provides a sea of clouds, punctuated by peaks. The climb itself is very easy. The stone stairway is well kept and there is a strong balustrade for the vertigo-prone. Along the way are several platforms where one can pause for a rest.

Peach Blossom Cave

This is the perfect place to visit after climbing the Heavenly Tour Peak. On returning 'to earth', turn right along the path beside the river. At times during the rainy season parts of this path are washed away; if you are not above a little paddle, you can always get through. The path is full of interest; there are little grottoes, butterflies, lace-cap hydrangeas, gardenias, providing a flower lover's paradise. Eventually one comes to a rock passage, where the adventure begins. Once inside, there is no visible exit and one seems to be trapped. Do not despair; follow on until there looms ahead a high grey stone wall with a magnificent tree growing up it, and a shaft of light illuminates the grotto floor. As one approaches the centre of the grotto a stone gateway comes into view on the right. Climb the few stairs and there before one is the secret garden, the Peach Blossom Cave.

During the Jin Dynasty (265–316) the famous poet Tao Qian wrote his classic *The Land of Peach Blossoms*. It told of a fictitious paradise, hidden in the mountains away from the world of turmoil and filled with ever blooming peach trees. Some say that after writing this article Tao Qian searched China to find his idyllic Peach Blossom Garden, eventually discovering it in Wuyi. Indeed, it is beautiful. One walks through a stone gateway into a flat valley planted with peach trees and surrounded by the sheer pleated peaks. Whilst standing by the stone gateway surveying this magical scene, look down. There are two stone benches, and, in between, a chessboard carved on another stone. Since the Song Dynasty the valley was a favourite abode of holy men and recluses, and at the far end of the garden stands the Daoist **Peach Blossom Temple** (Taoyuan Miao) dating from that time. The Main Hall, now a tea-room and vegetarian restaurant, is charming because of the way the rear part of the roof is slanted; it gives one a framed picture of bright green pine and bamboo on a canvas of a grey peak above. The inhabitants of this paradise are several elderly monks, one of whom has lived here for the past 30 years. They run the tea-room, restaurant and rooms for overnight guests. These are quite basic, but the absence of running water is made up by the pleasure of drawing it oneself from the crystal-clear Golden Brick Spring beside the temple.

Wuyi Palace

Wuyi Palace has stood at the First Twist of the Nine-twist Stream for at least a thousand years and probably much longer. Folklore suggests that Emperor Wudi (reigned 140–87 BC) had an altar built on the site to make offerings of dried fish to the Lord of Wuyi. Later a Daoist monastery was established on the site.

Although in a beautiful setting surrounded by fine trees (two laurels date from the Song Dynasty), the Wuyi Palace is in fact a drab grey building. At present it is used as a furniture store by CITS, their new hotel only a few minutes away. However, across the way is an attractive building named the **Ten-thousand Year Palace** which is well worth a look around. This palace is currently the home of a bamboo furniture workshop.

Water Screen Cave (Shuilian Dong)

To the north of the Nine-twist Stream is an area full of interesting walks and sights. Here the peaks are on a more intimate scale. A pleasant stroll along the road amongst them brings one, after some 20 minutes, to the **Nine-Dragon Den**. Here the landscape opens out into a canyon flanked by nine ridges (the nine dragons). The canyon is planted with tea bushes and some of the land is terraced. The tea produced here is called 'Big Red Robe'. This rather strange name dates from the Qing Dynasty: the tea was one of Emperor Qianlong's favourites, and so when sending it north to Beijing it was ceremoniously wrapped in auspicious red robes. This popular tea is reputed to have medicinal qualities. Today some 1,800 kilograms (4,000 pounds) are produced every year from this garden.

The walk up through the tea terraces brings one to **Dragon Bath Pool** and a deafening noise. A sheer yellow rock-face rises way above and, from its flat summit, drops a curtain of water, thundering into the circular pond. The pond is edged in stone and is a favourite place for the local ladies to do their washing.

A little way up the rock-face is a long, rectangular opening called the Water Screen Cave. From down below it seems to be an open space but, on climbing the steps and arriving at the terrace of the caves, one discovers it to be filled with a delightful old wooden building. Originally built as a Confucius temple during the Tang Dynasty, it became, later, in Song times, a Daoist temple and reputedly also had a period as a Buddhist temple. However, it is now a teahouse where it is also possible to spend the night. The tea served is grown here; usually there are several women sitting behind large round bamboo trays sifting the leaves. The annual production is just 45 kilograms (100 pounds). A rope attached to the cliff face higher up acts as a conduit for diverting a little of the pure water that cascades down past the terrace. When the kettle needs to be filled, someone merely holds it under the rope. The tea is indeed delicious, but even if one is not a tea lover, this is a magical place in which to linger.

Chong'an Town

Chong'an is a market town some ten kilometres (six miles) northeast of the Wuyi range. For most of the journey the road follows the Chong River. The mountains lie to the west of the road while, to the east, broad acres of farmland spread out. Just before you reach Chong'an a magnificent wooden bridge comes into sight, but to get to it you must go into town. The bridge is a 20-metre (66-foot) long construction

dating from the early Qing Dynasty. Its wooden superstructure, with complicated rafters, is completed with a 'pavilion roof' atop the middle sections. The whole structure is supported by stone wall buttresses. Nowadays it is shut to all but pedestrians. The early evening is a good time to go there. And there is always plenty of activity at the riverside: ducks being walked and vegetables washed for the evening meal. At the end of the day the pink light from the setting sun illuminates the old wood of the bridge and glistens on the water.

The centre of Chong'an has a splendid market, full of fresh vegetables, fish, fowl and fruit. In an alley off the market are several bamboo furniture factories as well as a bedding factory. In the middle of a warehouse stands several vast tables, on which are laid kapok quilts. At each table two men wield large wooden discs across the kapok to flatten and compact them.

The Chong'an County Museum has an interesting exhibit of one of the coffin boats from Wuyi. As in the Fuzhou Museum, there is a detailed photographic record of how archaeologists set about retrieving the coffin. Also exhibited are some objects from the Han city which has been excavated near Wuyi.

Han City

In 1959, the site of a Han-Dynasty (206 BC—AD 220) city was discovered near Wuyi. Excavation revealed a city of an irregular rectangular shape with a perimeter wall of some 2,500 metres (2,700 yards), ranging from two to six metres (6.6 to 20 feet) in height. The 'bones' of the city were well enough preserved to allow archaeologists to map out the whole area — drainage system, roads, sections of buildings, a cemetery and several workshops. Over 40,000 relics have been unearthed, such as pottery, iron and copper ware and agricultural equipment including a 15-kilogram (33-pound) iron ploughhead.

It is difficult to visit this archaeological site; technically it is only open to visitors with a permit. However, no one seems quite sure where the permit should be issued. The Cultural Bureau says Wuyi is the place and vice versa. Seasoned China travellers will be familiar with, and able to rise above, such frustrations. Even if one fails to obtain the correct entry permit, the Qing-Dynasty village beside the site is well worth a visit.

To reach the village (and the Han City) involves some seven or eight kilometres (4.3 or 5 miles) of bumping along a dirt road through paddy fields. At last the village comes in sight, hipped roofs rising above the yellow sandstone walls that surround it. Inside, the paved streets are narrow, punctuated at various intervals by a *pai* (the traditional roofed arch) and at times sections of the streets themselves are roofed. Most of the houses have wooden walls and balconies and there are plants everywhere. The village has that strange feeling of being untouched by world events; certainly the older generation is not used to seeing foreigners. One young visitor with flowing blond hair caused much puzzlement; why did this young face have the hair colour of an old woman? As the village is in the middle of rich farmland, it is a little like a giant farmyard with animals roaming everywhere. Villagers not out in the fields sort tea leaves or hull rice indoors. During wet weather the farmers all don the traditional straw cape and skirt; no hint of a plastic mackintosh is anywhere to be seen.

Wuyi Nature Reserve

This reserve was one of the favourite stamping grounds of the 19th-century European botanists. Father Jean-Pierre Armand David was a frequent visitor. Among the many plants that he discovered in China and that bear his name is the lovely 'handkerchief tree' (*Davidia involucrata*).

The drive southwest from Wuyi takes about an hour. The route is through a valley of beautifully manicured fields, most of them growing rice. Hamlets dot the fields and blue hills circle the scene. The last stretch of the journey goes through the beginning of the nature reserve. The small road runs beside a fast-flowing stream with a glorious array of flora all around: strong, tall Regale lilies (brought to Europe by E.H. Wilson); wild roses of many colours; white, lace-cap hydrangeas and wild azaleas. A stop along the road is well worthwhile just to take in the scene.

Further on, one arrives at the headquarters of the reserve. The area was designated in 1979, and is one of the six major reserves in China (there are also 106 minor ones). It covers a huge area, 95 percent of which is subtropical virgin forest, the remaining 5 percent set aside for buildings and roads. No hunting, shooting or indeed snake catching, no unauthorized wood cutting and no picking of flowers are allowed. Around 3,000 people live in the area — many grow tea, producing some 907 kilograms (2,000 pounds) each year. There is a research department, which attracts visiting scientists from overseas as well as from all over China. For the lay visitor there is an excellent exhibition hall. There is a wealth of wild fauna in the reserve, altogether some 400 species. The rarities include tiger, clouded leopard, howler monkey, horn toad and white-necked long-tailed pheasants. Illustrations of many of these species are on show, as well as unfriendly looking preserved snakes in bottles. There are some stuffed bears, and the collection of butterflies is stunning.

The reserve is also especially interesting to ornithologists as an important migratory stopping place for birds. It is possible for enthusiasts and wildlife groups to take three- or four-day field trips into the forest. Special permission and a schedule have to be pre-arranged.

Snake Zoo

Near the Wuyi Mountain Nature Reserve is the Snake Zoo; this was set up in 1980 both to exhibit the reptiles and to conduct research on venom. There are some six tons of living snakes on view here; and their enclosures are designed to resemble natural habitat. In winter, the zoo trains hibernating snakes by hypnosis to kill rats and then return undisturbed into hibernation.

Attached to the zoo is the research institute, which concentrates on finding new drugs to treat snake bite. There is a hospital and outpatient department incorporated here and it is highly regarded as a treatment centre. There is also a restaurant here which specializes in snake dishes, extremely popular with overseas Chinese.

Quanzhou

Quanzhou was the world's second largest port during the Middle Ages. Today the bustle of big-time commerce is gone, leaving a city of 140,000 people (medium-small by China's standards) with a rich cultural heritage. Quanzhou stands on the north bank of the Jinjiang River's lower reaches, a few miles from the river's mouth. The climate is mild year round, hence the nickname 'Wenling' (warm hill).

The town was founded in 711. Because of its position near the mouth of the Jinjiang River — which flows into a vast natural harbour — Quanzhou quickly developed as a port. It reached the peak of its prosperity during the Song and Yuan Dynasties. A special customs office was set up to deal with foreign ships in 1086 and, by the 12th and 13th centuries, a large number of Western merchants were based here, living in an area to the south of the city. Historians are now agreed that Zaytun, the 'great emporium' frequently mentioned in contemporary Western and Arabic texts, was Quanzhou. The Chinese histories also describe the city's international flavour: 'On the rising tide, commercial ships come in from all countries'. Quanzhou's most renowned Western visitor was Marco Polo. He had been entrusted with accompanying a princess from the court of Kublai Khan to the Middle East where she was to be married. In typically expansive style he describes the trade: 'at this city is the port . . . to which all the ships from India come with many goods and dear, and namely with many precious stones of great value and with many pearls both large and good. And moreover I tell you that the great Kaan receives in this port very great duty.' Along with merchants came missionaries, both Christian and Muslim. Records indicate that several 14th-century bishops and Mohammed's third and fourth disciples visited Quanzhou.

The prosperity of the 13th and early 14th centuries ended with the Ming ousting the Yuan Dynasty in 1368. The Ming allowed the port of Quanzhou to silt up, and by 1644, when they were overthrown by the Qing, Xiamen — with her superb natural harbour — had usurped Quanzhou's position.

Along with the other parts of Fujian's coast, Quanzhou suffered periodic raids by Japanese pirates and direct military attack during the Sino-Japanese War. Quanzhou today is peaceful and although it has not in relative terms regained the prosperity of its Yuan-Dynasty heyday (its port takes only 3,000 tons; visitors are not allowed at the Naval Section), it nevertheless thrives as a market town surrounded by fertile farmland.

Quanzhou is not on the rail system. Several buses make the 196-kilometre (121-mile) journey from Fuzhou and the 106-kilometre (66-

mile) trip from Xiamen daily. Quanzhou is also a stop for the through bus Fuzhou-Xiamen-Hong Kong.

Hotels in Quanzhou

Golden Fountain Hotel
Baiyuanqing Chi Pang
tel. 5078, fax. 4388

金泉饭店
白源清池旁

Eight double, Rmb100; 78 twin-rooms, Rmb80−100; five suites, Rmb250. Banquet hall, Fujianese, Cantonese and Western restaurants; hairdresser; IDD from lobby. (Amex, MasterCard, Federal)

Well located in the courtyard of the Overseas Chinese Mansion, just a few minutes' walk from the centre of town and overlooking the lake, this new Hong Kong-joint venture is plush but dirty. Be warned: a Western breakfast ordered the night before does not necessarily materialize in the morning.

Overseas Chinese Mansion
Baiyuanqing Chi Pang
tel. 2192
cable 5132

华侨大厦
白源清池旁

70 double, Rmb50 for overseas Chinese and Rmb61 for foreigners per person; 100 triple-rooms, Rmb40 and Rmb53; 15 suites, Rmb72. Banquet hall, Fujianese and Cantonese restaurants, with Western breakfast served on the groud floor; IDD; disco. (Amex, MasterCard, Visa, Federal)

The lifts are slow, and the cold water is hardly more reliable than the hot. The restaurants are as dirty as the rest of the hotel, but the food is good and the beer is cold. Location is a plus, but not for light sleepers, as Hui'an produce vendors begin to arrive.at the market in the street below at 4 am.

Restaurants in Quanzhou

Mantang Hong
3−5 Zhongshan Lu (Middle section)
tel. 2887

满堂红
中山路3−5号

Situated one storey up in the old part of town, this restaurant is very basic, but the tablecloths are clean, the beer is cold and the food delicious. The Quanzhou variant of Fujianese food, as served here, includes *jiaozi* (dumplings), steamed crabs, and a mixture of

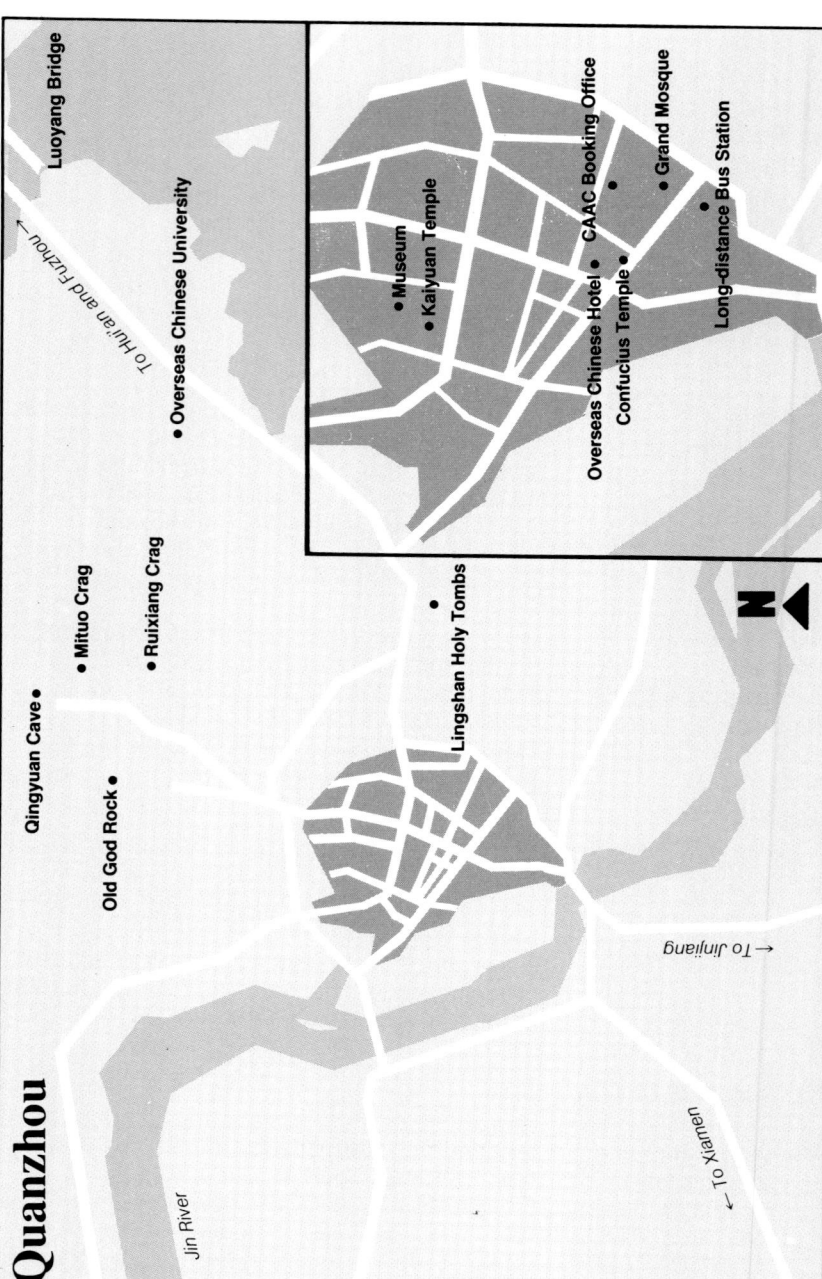

Quanzhou

Jin River

To Hui'an and Fuzhou →

Luoyang Bridge

Qingyuan Cave ●

● Mituo Crag

Old God Rock ●

● Ruixiang Crag

● Overseas Chinese University

Lingshan Holy Tombs ●

← To Jinjiang

← To Xiamen →

● Museum
● Kaiyuan Temple

Overseas Chinese Hotel ●
● CAAC Booking Office

Confucius Temple ●

● Grand Mosque

Long-distance Bus Station ●

N

glutinous rice, gingko seeds and mushrooms wrapped and steamed in bamboo leaves. Everything has garlic. Choose a window table for the view. Open noon−2 pm and 6−8 pm.

Baiyuan Jiujia
Cultural Palace
tel. 2859, 2178

白源酒家
文化宫

Located at the Cultural Palace, a pleasant stroll around the lake from the Overseas Chinese Mansion, this restaurant serves good Quanzhou-style food. Open 10.30 am−2 pm and 5.30−9 pm.

The Arts in Quanzhou

Quanzhou owes its rich cultural tradition in part to the turmoil of the Five Dynasties (907−60). For 53 years the north was split into five kingdoms, the south into another ten. Hence many people from the north migrated towards the southern coast with the intention of leaving China. However, finding in Quanzhou a pleasant climate, attractive surroundings and a growing international community, many of the literati settled here.

Quanzhou still has an active community of writers, poets, playwrights and painters working here. There is a flourishing group of modern as well as traditional painters. Puppetry (see page 78) is one of the city's oldest and most respected art forms. The puppets are the marionette-type (literally in Chinese 'string-suspending puppet').

Quanzhou opera is of national significance, as an early unadulterated variety is still performed here. Gaojia Opera is perhaps the most popular in the area. This 'new' style dates from the middle Qing Dynasty (only some 200 years old). Earlier, during the Ming Dynasty, it became popular for bands of players, dressed in costumes, to join religious processions on festival days and to perform quick sketches. These shows grew in popularity, and when the scenes expanded into full-length productions, Gaojia Opera eventually evolved. It has also, over time, borrowed from other styles, but the music is strongly southern — incorporating local folk tunes, melodies from puppet scores — and it is sung in the local dialect. The majority of the plays performed are traditional, although the repertoire does include a few contemporary scripts. The clown is a key figure in Quanzhou theatre: there are over 20 clown classifications in Gaojia Opera.

Shopping in Quanzhou

Quanzhou's main streets have covered walkways, so the avid shopper is protected against both rain and sun. Wonderful window-shopping can be done here. In fact, if staying at the Overseas Chinese Hotel with a south-facing bedroom one is bound to be woken by the chatter of the farmers arriving to set out their produce in Middle Market. To get there, turn right out of the hotel, take the next right and the entrance to the market is on the left. This market is stunning, a feast for the eye and for the camera. Many of the hawkers are Hui'an women (see page 81), who wear their unique dress, often with gay floral scarves or bright yellow conical-shapped hats; in summer many of them will show bare midriffs. Even the local Quanzhou ladies dress their hair beautifully, with flowers encircling a bun secured by a chopstick or with a little posy of flowers jauntily pinned to the side of the head. The produce in the market is beautifully presented. The first section is covered and contains fish in all shapes and sizes, meat, vegetables, and eggs — of hen, duck, quail and pigeon — displayed in pyramids. There are several restaurants which do brisk breakfast trade; instead of congee (rice gruel) they sell a sort of hot-pot accompanied by long twisted doughnuts. There is a stall selling ready-made dumplings to take home as well as all types of beancurd. If one walks diagonally across the market and out the opposite left-hand corner one finds more stalls. Here all manner of pickled goods are stored in wooden vats. Gradually the food stalls give way to household goods, particularly piles of pottery cooking pots. By the bridge are the flower sellers, who offer ready-made hair decorations, such as a circle of marigolds or jasmine, or mixed nosegays for temple offerings.

To visit the main shopping area, ask a pedicab to go to the Nanmen Department Store at 274 Zhongshan Nan Lu. This has a wide selection of enamelware and — for the fashion conscious — a fine line in striped leg warmers. Nearby, at 270 Zhongshan Nan Lu, is a snack shop which specializes in sweet dumpling soup. The dumplings, formed by pounding rice flour with sesame seeds and sugar, are delicious. Although served all year round this soup is a traditional New Year's dish. Further along the road, at number 304, is the CGC Trading Company. This is a joint venture with Hong Kong; much of the stock is imported and the goods are better displayed than in many Chinese stores. A Friendship Store upstairs accepts both both RMB and FEC. Opposite number 358 is Guoying Yuan Fang Fandian (it does not have a number of its own). This is another, slightly smarter, snack shop with banquet facilities upstairs. At 506 is the Arts and Crafts Store where a good selection of Fujian crafts, including lacquer goods and cork

carvings, are on sale. The road soon becomes Zhongshan Lu
Zhongduan (Middle section). Whichever way you turn at this
intersection the shops continue much the same. At 13 Huaxiang Jie is
the Embroidery and Handicraft Factory of Quanzhou which produces,
in addition to embroidery, lacquer ducks, silk flowers, bamboo
baskets, clay figures — all the goods that you will find on sale in the
Arts and Crafts Store.

Sights in Quanzhou

Kaiyuan Temple

This beautiful temple has a history of some 1,300 years. According to
the legend, in 680, during the Tang Dynasty, the prefect of the area
(for Quanzhou town was not founded until 711) dreamed that a monk
approached him asking for land on which to build a temple. The
prefect answered that he would grant the request only on the condition
that the mulberry tree in his garden became covered with lotus flowers.
Indeed, the next day, not only was the mulberry tree covered in lotus
flowers but the very same monk appeared with a request for land to
build a temple. The prefect offered his house immediately as the
temple site.

The Kaiyuan Temple is in the old part of the city to the northwest,
a pleasant 30-minute stroll or a short pedicab ride from the Overseas
Chinese Hotel. At the temple entrance is a small pavilion which houses
the Ziyun (Purple Cloud) screen. On the other side of the screen the
temple comes into view at the far end of a vast granite courtyard. It is
walled by clipped bougainvillaea and hibiscus hedges, complete with
moon gates and circular windows, and by a row of banyan trees, some
800 years old. In summer, groups of old men sit at stone tables in the
shade of the spreading trees playing chess or cards. To the west and
east the upper storeys of the stone pagodas rise above the hedge.

The big Ziyun Hall (Main Hall) sits on a stone dais, around which
are carvings of animals. The temple itself has a double roof structure,
but what is unusual is that the space between the two roofs is filled
with open slates, giving the top roof a floating appearance and allowing
extra light inside the building. A complicated beam structure supports
the bottom roof. At the points where the roof beams meet the wall the
floating illusion is repeated and contributes to the ethereal feeling of
the building as a whole. Inside the large main hall sit the Five
Direction Buddhas who are in charge of the five divisions of the world
— north, south, east, west and central. The roofs are held up by 100
stone pillars, two of which, at the centre in front of the Buddhas, are

beautifully carved. Twenty-four of the pillars are topped with celestial musicians; each has the body of a human, the hooves of a horse and the wings of a bird. They appear to support the roofs with their heads. The ceiling iself is divided into squares decorated with bats around the symbol for longevity.

Leave the Main Hall by its rear door, turn left and there poking over a wall is a branch of the original 1,300-year-old mulberry tree said to have been covered with lotus blossoms. Sixty years ago it was struck by lightning and split into three. This section is supported by the wall; it actually rests on two charming stone fish. One of the stones beside the tree bears the emperor's edict, 'As this tree is very old and has given birth to lotus flowers, it is ordered that no damage be done to it.'

At the far end of the courtyard, behind the Main Hall, stands the Ordination Hall. In the centre of the hall on a granite dais is a statue of the Goddess of Mercy, her 1,000 hands outstretched. Above her head the rafters form a cupola. She is protected by 32 statues, including those of eight ferocious black guards with Indian features: evidence of Quanzhou's international status during the Song Dynasty. Four beautifully carved corner stones hold up the dais and are worth a glance. In a small building behind the Ordination Hall is the temple shop where one can buy rubbings, painting and calligraphy equipment and miscellaneous pieces of porcelain. A drawer serves as a till and a candle balanced on an upturned cup provides the only light. In the shop courtyard two withered pine trees stand guard.

Walk back along the east side of the Ordination Hall, past a collection of Song and Tang stone carvings (many of which do not belong to the Kaiyuan Temple but are here for safe-keeping). Turn left through an arch past a shop selling postcards, and a little further on the left is a beautiful wooden door with finely carved stone pillars on either side. The courtyard within is worth a brief look, not only for its stone carving but for its topiary, and a bougainvillaea trained into the shape of a pavilion.

Ancient Boat Exhibition

Next, to the east, is a museum which contains the remains of a Song-Dynasty ocean-going ship and some of its cargo. The ship was discovered in 1974 by fishermen at Houzhu some ten kilometres (six miles) downstream from Quanzhou. The ship was embedded in the mud of the riverbed, which acted as a preservative. Nevertheless, only about a third of the vessel remains. Three types of wood were used in the construction: pine, camphor and cryptomeria. It seems remarkably small by modern standards. Near the keel is the ship's talisman, a small copper disc called a 'longevity hole'. Evidence of the seafaring trade of the day are provided by some Islamic stone carvings dating from the 11th and 12th centuries. Also shown are arched tomb doors bearing Islamic inscriptions and the Chinese characters for 'foreign guest tablet'. There is a tablet describing the life of a Quanzhou man who had been sent to Hormuz in 1299 as an envoy.

If the ship seems small from eye level, looking at it from the gallery above it is easier to imagine it sailing the trade routes. Rooms off the gallery exhibit the remains of the cargo as well as sundry other items of the ship's contents, including sheep's bones and teeth (the crew's food would have been taken on alive), pottery bowls, jewellery, chessmen, money, rattan hats, the cargo manifest (a wooden board with the characters for the different shippers or consignees of the cargo) and medicine, much of which when analyzed was found to be similar to many of today's potions. There is a model reconstruction of the ship as well as a photographic record of the find.

Leave the museum and walk towards the **East Pagoda**, originally built of wood in 865, and later rebuilt in brick. The outside of the pagoda is carved with Buddha images and other religious figures such as *arhats*. The relief carving is considered superior to that on the **West Pagoda**. The original West Pagoda, like its sister, was built of wood and was first completed in 916. From the top of both is a fine view of Quanzhou city and the surrounding countryside.

Old God Rock

At the foot of Qingyuan Mountain, a few miles north of Quanzhou, sits a majestic stone figure of Lao Zi, the philosopher. Lao Zi lived during the Warring States period (475–221 BC) and was one of the originators of the Daoist belief (it cannot strictly be considered a religion). Sculpted out of the mountain, this statue is thought to date from the tenth century (Tang Dynasty). Originally the statue was covered by a Daoist temple which was destroyed by an earthquake during the Ming Dynasty. One approaches the statue following a granite path through the fields, beneath a granite arch, up a stone flight of steps; there gazing down sits the wise, old sage.

This is also a good starting point for those who wish to visit the other places of interest on Qingyuan Mountain, like the **Ruixiang** and **Mituo Crags**. The path up into the mountain starts behind the Lao Zi statue. It is probably best to take a picnic; however, there is a small restaurant which serves noodles and other basic fare near Mituo Crag.

The Grand Mosque (Qingjing Si)

Five minutes' walk south of the Overseas Chinese Hotel, on Tumen Jie, is the Grand Mosque surrounded by high granite walls. It was built in 1009. Beside the Worshipping Hall is a small courtyard house; one building is used as a museum. The museum walls are covered in pictures and explanations of the history of Islam in Quanzhou and the surrounding area. During the Song and Yuan Dynasties there were six mosques in the city. Today some 400 Muslims use the mosque. Arabic is used for the sermon and prayers but the imam teaches in Chinese.

Fujian Puppets

The skill of a master puppeteer requires that 'one breath tell a thousand ancient tales and two hands create the dance of a million soldiers'. This skill is a legacy of generations — the stories, movements and stagecraft passed down from father to son.

Wooden and clay funereal figures dating from the Zhou Dynasty (1066−256 BC) are believed to be China's first puppets. These figures were effigies of the deceased's relatives and servants who were placed in the tomb to watch over their master. As part of the funeral rites the shaman (medicine man) is thought to have manipulated these jointed figures so they appeared to take on the spirit of the deceased.

The fact that they were popularly believed to have the ability to influence the spirit world may be one reason for the ever increasing interest in puppetry. It was thought that it was easy for wandering spirits to possess puppets because they were so life-like. For safety's sake at the end of a performance they were stored in a secure basket, the head apart from the body, and the clown (the mascot of puppetry) always placed on top. The art of puppetry sustained its popularity until 1966 when the classical form virtually disappeared with the onset of the Cultural Revolution. By 1979 most groups had reassembled, though sadly some techniques were lost in the interim because little had been written down and some of the masters had died.

Today Fujian Province is the home of China's most famed puppet troupes, practising both the string and glove forms. It is thought that Quanzhou became a marionette centre during the tenth century when it served as the exit port for the tide of migrants from China's unsettled north. The language and music used nowadays in Quanzhou's traditional puppet plays date from that time. Today new plays have been added to the traditional repertoire of 300. There are, however, some basic differences in modern marionette performances. The scenery is now three-dimensional, and the puppets can be controlled by as many as 30 strings. It takes many years for a puppeteer to become a master for he must know all the plays by heart, and indeed all masters teach groups of.

Some two kilometres (1.2 miles) east of the city are the **Lingshan Holy Tombs**. The bodies of two Muslim sages who came to preach in Quanzhou during the Tang Dynasty are said to be buried here. The setting is beautiful but it is not a particularly interesting site to visit.

Confucius Temple

Just beside the Overseas Chinese Hotel is an early Song Confucius Temple, one of the best preserved in the country. The temple has an

students. The skill of a marionettist is clearly displayed by the walk of his puppet. The style of a puppet's walk is highly individual, and the skilled puppeteer can convey not only the sex but the mood of a puppet by its 'body language'.

The art of glove puppetry (also known as sack puppetry and puppetry-on-palm) remained the same for centuries, and it was only changed in the past 50 years. Originally, the figures measured eight inches tall, but now they have been enlarged to 14 inches Like that of marionettes, the comportment of the puppets is all important. Martial arts shows offer the best potential for glove puppets to display their skills. (It is impossible to achieve the strength and determination of movement with a marionette whose feet float lightly across the stage.)

One of the most important aspects of the puppet, whether the glove or marionette type, is in the carving of the head and hands. Historically, the puppet carvers of Fujian have been highly respected and their products the most sought after in China. Camphor is a favourite wood used to carve these pieces; according to one master it is fine-grained, not easily cracked and emits a delicate fragrance which was supposed to repel insects and reduce sweaty odours. Little tricks are used to convey character: different eye-sizes and an extended ridge above the eyes, for instance, so that when the puppet moves the audience sitting below will notice a change of expression and much else. The carvers model their puppets on local faces, the water carrier and snack vendor being particular favourites of Quanzhou's most renowned carver. One head will take four to five weeks to complete; after carving it has to be polished, painted, and have its hair and head-dress added. The clothes which the puppet wears are predominantly silk and especially embroidered. It is quite usual to see groups of women in Fujian chatting on their doorsteps as they embroider these exquisite pieces.

A visit to see any of the Fujian puppet groups is an enormous pleasure. The dialogue is likely to be in one of the local dialects so your chances of following it are perhaps limited — little matter, however; the performances are action-packed and superbly expressive, and often there is a helpful neighbour to whisper the story outline to you.

interesting beam structure, which is apparently designed to protect buildings against earthquakes. (Quanzhou is in an earthquake zone and has recorded one measuring eight on the Richter Scale.) The fact that these buildings still stand is testimony to the engineering skills of China's architects some 1,000 years ago. The vaulted ceiling is painted with phoenix and dragons; sadly, the east side was bombed by the Japanese, so part of the painting was lost although the building stood.

The building is run by the Quanzhou Cultural Bureau. At night, the building forms a beautiful backdrop for cultural events. The hotel desk should have information on performances. The street outside is turned into a 'night market', selling clothing and goods of no special interest to an overseas visitor; nonetheless, it provides a splendid opportunity to observe the night-life of the city.

Sights outside Quanzhou

Luoyang Bridge (Luoyang Qiao)

Continuing on the Fuzhou road one comes to the Luoyang Bridge. This old stone bridge now serves only pedestrians, since a new car bridge spans the Luoyang River a few hundred yards to the north. It was built during the Song Dynasty between 1053 and 1059. Stone slabs rest on 49 pillars: today they are topped by a new tarmac surface and are difficult to see. Luoyang Bridge in fact traverses a tidal inlet, and it is well worth visiting at low tide when the fishermen are out in force working knee-deep in the mud flats which they have divided into small squares. Some of the fields are covered in strange little pyramid mudbricks which act as greenhouses to protect the growing shellfish. The fishermen also have flat wooden implements to smooth the mud; they wait for bubbles revealing the whereabouts of their potential catch. These flat 'skis' are also used to carry other tools around: sometimes one sees them being whisked across the mud from one fisherman to another.

Hui'an County

The dress of the women from Hui'an County is so spectacular — they wear bright reds, greens, blues topped off with, say, a sparkling yellow hat — that one would think that they belonged to an exotic minority tribe; in fact they are Han Chinese. Local folklore has it that the dress dates back to the Song Dynasty when an official named Li Wenhui ruled Xiaosuo island. He fell in love with a pretty village girl whom he wished to marry. When she refused him, her arms and legs were bound and she was forced to go through with the ceremony. Later when their eldest daughter was to marry the mother dressed her in an outfit which recalled the circumstances of her own unhappy marriage: a short loose blouse and bare midriff as reminders of her dishevelled clothes; the embroidered squares recalling the patches with which she had mended them; and the bands of pattern around the bottom of the sleeves and trousers symbolizing the rope with which she had been trussed. However, there seems to be no satisfactory explanation of the head-dress, which is probably the most intriguing part of the costume. The hair is often piled up in a bun (sometimes it is plaited into pigtails), a long stick put through it horizontally so that when a floral headscarf is placed on top it sticks out each side. The two ends of the scarf are then tied at the point of the chin, turning the whole effect into a triangle, with a hat placed on top. Hui'an women wear this scarf until the age of 35 — part of a tradition which is only now breaking down.

Until recently, all marriages were always arranged by the families. Once married the bride and groom were allowed to spend their first night together; thereafter she would return home, only visiting her husband on high days and holidays until she became pregnant, then she would move in with her husband's family. Today, the young girls are beginning to disregard these old-fashioned rules and sneak out to meet their husbands at dead of night. However, as they keep their scarves on during these night-time rendezvous, husband and wife often pass in the street without recognizing each other.

Hui'an County lies northwest of Quanzhou and is also known as Granite County. Travelling from Putian southwest to Quanzhou, one finds that the landscape suddenly changes from fertile farmland to arid rocky scrub punctuated with quarries and granite. In fact granite appears everywhere — on houses, telegraph poles, fences and roofs. The effect is quite extraordinary. Many Hui'an women work alongside men on construction sites, but some of them have laid down their shovels and taken up crafts more in keeping with their costume, such as drawn-work embroidery and bamboo weaving. Nevertheless, the Hui'an people are still best known for their exquisite stone carving. In the town of Luoyang just before the famous bridge (see page 81) is a stone-carving factory which is well worth a visit. The masons chip away at vast pieces of granite; much of the work is for ancient monuments under restoration, although some is for private customers, usually overseas Chinese. They also produce a rather fascinating new product — the slate portrait. The craftsman works from a photograph of the subject and, with tremendous precision, reproduces the image on a slate by millions of little dots. The end product is almost a total likeness. The women also play their part in this local industry — when

the granite arrives at the factory from the quarry, it is these versatile
and industrious women who unload it. Hui'an carving is to be found at
all the famous monuments in Fujian — the stone pillars at the Kaiyuan
Temple are one example — and in other parts of China: all the carving
in the Mao Zedong Mausoleum in Beijing is Hui'an work.

Although Hui'an has also lost many of its indigenous people over
the years to the waves of emigration from the province, a number of
schemes were started in the 1950s to bring more of the arid, unfertile
land under cultivation and the county is no longr so poor. Now
sugarcane is grown in the 1,300 hectares (3,200 acres) reclaimed from
the northern Quanzhou Bay. The adjacent sugarcane factory can
produce 500 tons of refined sugar per day. By means of a complicated
irrigation system, the Linxi River is now able to water 2,000 hectares
(5,000 acres) of otherwise unproductive land.

Shishi and its Surroundings

On the way to Shishi, China's extraordinary boom town, stop off in
Chen Dai, the home of some 15,000 Muslims, who are known in China
as 'Hui'. Attracted by the great seaport of Quanzhou, many Muslims
migrated from the Silk Road down to the Quanzhou area during the
13th and 14th centuries. Chen Dai itself, however, was founded a short
time later in the early Ming Dynasty. During the Cultural Revolution
(1966–76) this community was forced to cease any public show of
religion, and had to use a 'family hall' rather than a mosque for
religious occasions. Happily today the situation is changed and the
construction of a mosque is planned.

Also worth a visit here is a charming building, a Hui people's
historical hall, built in the Ming Dynasty. The entrance looks like that
of a temple with an imposing gate but it is in fact a square courtyard —
the shape of the character for 'Hui'. Today this building is used as an
historical museum, charting the successes and frustrations of the local
Muslim community. Ironically, the majority of the inhabitants seem to
be pig farmers; indeed some of them even eat pork.

The drive from Chen Dai to Shishi takes one through Jinjiang
County, which, like Hui'an County, has a desolate landscape with
occasional patches of scrub or cultivated land. As the road nears
Shishi, large ornate armchair graves start to appear. Many overseas
Chinese choose to come home to be buried. It is quite extraordinary
that this town of 80,000 people, set in the midst of infertile land with
poor communications, should have become such a roaring commercial
success. There is no railway; the town is 30 kilometres (19 miles) from
the sea, and there is only a bad country road to connect it to the

outside world. Perhaps in a curious way the basis of its success lies in its geographic position. Because they could not make a living on land, vast numbers of people were forced to emigrate (there are some half a million in the Philippines alone). When they were successful in their new countries, they started to send money and goods back to Shishi, which allowed those left at home to take up manufacturing and, more recently, private enterprise.

Today the town is an entrepreneur's dream: the main street buzzes with activity and commerce. There are some 3,000 registered — and probably hundreds of unregistered — private retail enterprises as well as 500 collective manufacturing operations producing anything from bras (Love Flower brand) to rubber tubing. But Shishi is a town with few public services: there are no parks, and there are not enough schools to accommodate the student population, so several new ones have been sponsored by rich overseas compatriots. The bus station, opened in 1986, provides a good example of the local lust for commerce — it has been taken over by stall holders, and the buses still pick up passengers on street corners. 'Give a five-year-old child two eggs,' goes the local saying, 'and she will hit the street and turn a profit.'

The town boasts 64 hotels to accommodate visiting traders. There is the Overseas Chinese Mansion run by China Travel Service. The majority of the clientèle are compatriots returning to visit their families. The restaurant serves delicious food: *mangetout* (snow peas) are one of the area's few farming successes and indeed they are sweet and tasty. Shishi noodles are thin and traditionally mixed with squid, pork and cabbage.

Longevity Pagoda (Gusao Ta)

The Longevity Pagoda is near Shishi and well worth a visit. Follow the road southeast towards the sea until you arrive at a military camp. Continue through the camp, then wind up a paved road. The road goes through a barren landscape dominated by huge grey rocks, past a vast quarry (all the local houses are built of this grey stone) and eventually comes to an end. The pagoda is on the left at the top of a steep stone path, perched on rock. A stone stairway leads one past a modern pavilion and through scrubby vegetation dotted with lovely wild flowers. The highest point for miles around, the exposed, windy site commands a stunning view of the surrounding countryside and the sea far below. During the Song Dynasty (960–1279) it was used as a beacon by sailors; the present structure dates from 790 and itself replaced an earlier pagoda. It is a five-storey hexagonal building with balconies on each floor; a little dagoba crowns the roof. Everything is stone — even the roofs — and the style is plain; a pillar at each corner provides the only decoration. Inside is a single, floorless space: four stone beams run across from wall to wall, forming a diamond within the hexagon, presumably to keep the pagoda from collapsing inwards. A small Buddha image sits in a niche. A stairway within the walls of the pagoda enables one to climb to each level; it is an effort repaid many fold by the view from the balconies above.

After you leave the pagoda, follow the road back down through the military camp, turn left out of the gate, and on the left in the fields is a village dominated by a grandiose mansion, built in the 1950s by an overseas Chinese from the Philippines. Great verandahs surround the core of the house, a turret marks the front, and a four-tiered cupola tops the roof. Today it is occupied by several families — apparently tenants of the owner, though the latter died some time ago and no-one claims the house. The countryside of Fujian is dotted with these grand houses, but they are particularly prevalent around Shishi. Usually family members live in them, and sometimes their original owners return from overseas to retire. This particular village boasts several other large houses (though none quite so grand) and other surprises. Around the back of the big house, in some outlying buildings, one may find a group of ladies doing exquisite embroidery called 'couching'. A length of red silk is stretched on a wooden frame; for some of the work brightly coloured silk thread is used, for the rest, gold thread. The gold thread — of varying thicknesses — outlines a motif such as a dragon or butterfly. The work produced in this particular workshop is made into the panels on traditional wedding dresses.

Another interesting village to visit is **Shangdi** in Jinjiang County. If driving from Quanzhou to Xiamen (via Shishi and the Longevity Pagoda), one should stop just past Shangdi's centre, where there is a large school on the left. A walk through the playground and down the alley where the other side leads to the back of a charming Buddhist temple dating from the Tang Dynasty (518–907). The Buddha image is missing, but several *arhats* (disciples) are in place. Great gold dragons curl around the central stone pillars, and on the roof are carved animals and human figures. In one of the side rooms there is an old sedan chair covered in plastic sheeting. However, the most intriguing aspect of small farmyard temples such as this is the spectacle of daily worship. Sometimes the incense smoke is so thick that it is hard to see from one side of the hall to the other. Periodically, the relative calm is shattered by firecrackers set off to frighten away ghosts; they leave one's eardrums singing and add to the sense of bizarre worldliness.

Zhangzhou

Zhangzhou is an ancient city with a population today of some 300,000. It is set in the middle of Fujian's richest alluvial plain on the lower reaches of the Jiulong River (Nine Dragons River).

The city was founded by General Chen Yuanguang some 1,300 years ago in the Tang Dynasty. The general, both a scholar and strategist, had realized the potential of the Zhangzhou area, with its fast flowing Jiulong River, easy access to the sea and its rich alluvial plain. A prefecture was set up and General Chen Yuanguang became Zhangzhou's first governor. He was a successful administrator, and soon the area was flourishing. Until the 18th century Zhangzhou remained southern Fujian's principal port, exporting silk, chiffon and sugar. But trade slackened as the river began to silt up and business went to Xiamen. Today Zhangzhou has a rail link to the coast and is once again a prosperous city producing vast quantities of flowers and fruit, particularly lychees, *longyan* (Dragon-Eye), pineapples and bananas. There is also a highly productive sugar refinery here. The city is an important cultural centre, too: Fujian's famous hand puppetry originated in Zhangzhou's Song-Dynasty period.

The Fuzhou-Xiamen express train does not run all the way to Zhangzhou but does stop at Guokang, 11.5 kilometres (seven miles) northeast of Zhangzhou. Buses from Xiamen are more frequent and faster, and there are through buses from Fuzhou. Dongshan is reached by bus from Zhangzhou.

Hotels in Zhangzhou

Zhangzhou Overseas Chinese Mansion
38 Yan'an Bei Lu
tel. 3614
tlx. 4357

漳州华侨大厦
延安北路38号

Dormitory, Rmb6; 38 double rooms, Rmb40−78, two suites. Banquet hall, Fujianese/Cantonese and Western restaurants, coffee shop; clinic; massage. (Amex, Mastercard, Visa, Federal)

This clean, old-fashioned hotel supplies mosquito nets in the evening, even though rooms are air-conditioned. Rocks and a fountain grace the garden, which fills with lilies in May. Food in the restaurant is very good, and the shop has a surprising stock, including Nescafé (decaffeinated and regular), Beaujolais red, Blanc de Blanc and Stoloichnaya vodka.

**Zhangzhou
Guesthouse**
4 Shengli Lu
tel. 4761, 3429

漳州宾馆
胜利路4号

Eight single rooms, Rmb39; 160 double rooms, Rmb42; 14 suites, Rmb120. Banquet hall, four Chinese (including Fujianese) and one Western restaurant; hairdresser, conference rooms; garden. (Amex)

This old-style hotel, with all rooms in small buildings, is a joint venture with a Hong Kong trading company.

Restaurants in Zhangzhou

Fucheng Restaurant
Shixing Bei Lu

府程饭店
始兴北路

Located beside Zhongshan Park, this inexpensive restaurant serves Fujian food with Zhangzhou specialities, one of which is a delicious open-face omelette made using duck eggs and little oysters, with corn and potato flour mixed in. Seafood is fresh and excellent, and are served with style. (Local oysters are frozen and exported to Hong Kong.) The restaurant, comprising about 30 stalls with bamboo tables and chairs, provides superb value. Open all day.

Hai Wei Guan
Yan'an Nan Lu
tel. 3679

海味馆
延安南路

This fairly basic restaurant is opposite the Confucius Temple and the new primary school. In its upstairs dining room it serves seafood, Coca Cola and beer. Delicious smells waft from the bakery next door. This is an interesting place to go for lunch, as it is in the middle of a market.

**Nanshan Temple
Vegetarian
Restaurant**
Nanshan Temple
tel. 4959

南山寺素菜馆
南山寺

Run by the Buddhist Association, this 150-seat restaurant serves outstanding food. Eggplant with beancurd shaped like tortellini in a light sweet-and-sour sauce is good, as are the dish with green beans and snow peas (a speciality of Zhangzhou) and another dish with carved phoenix vegetable. There is also a peanut soup served in individual Yixing pots. Beer and Royal Jelly grape wine are available.

Shopping in Zhangzhou

Strolling around the market streets of Zhangzhou is the most entertaining way to shop. The main market street, Beiqiao Shichang, is a mere five-minute walk from the Overseas Chinese Mansion. Turn left out of the hotel along Yan'an Lu, an interesting street itself with an excellent noodle shop, a small department store and an arts and crafts shop. Take the second right (or any of the right turns thereafter) which leads into a web of market streets. The main market street is heralded by two stone gateways with double curved roofs and carved stone figures on the pillars, which date from the Ming Dynasty. Here one finds an interesting mixture of food stalls, eating places, children's library, a puncture mending service and in general plenty of opportunities to acquire knick-knacks for those at home. In the adjacent Qingnian Lu is a delightful Protestant church where services are held every Sunday. This was built around the turn of the century, survived the Cultural Revolution unscathed, and today is lovingly cared for by a group of elderly ladies. The church is right beside the Babao Ink Paste Factory (see below). And, next to the factory entrance, is a shop filled with interesting bric-a-brac, paint brushes, paintings, lacquer work and so on. The Catholic Church the other side of the block was built by the Spanish in 1980. It has Gothic-style windows and, although in good repair inside, has several trees growing out of its turrets. The congregation can number up to 500.

The easiest and most interesting way to buy the arts and crafts of Zhangzhou is to visit the factories where they are made (see below).

Arts and Crafts in Zhangzhou

Painting Zhangzhou is famous for its painters. The District Cultural Bureau has a gallery where the artists who belong to the Zhangzhou Painting Institute exhibit their work. Half of the sale proceeds go to the artist, half to the gallery. The works shown are mostly traditional brush paintings and calligraphy: there are, however, some modern pieces. Some painters are happy to show their work at home: those interested should ask at their hotel.

Local Opera Zhangzhou boasts four types of indigenous opera: Talking and Singing-Song, Wooden Image Opera, Chao Opera and Zhangzhou Opera. All of these are performed in the local dialect. Zhangzhou Opera, with its 300-year history, is an amalgam of folk dance and other dramatic traditions. Over the past 40 years the librettos and the stories have been enriched and, like all Chinese

Zhangzhou

Railway Station

Yan'an Bei Lu

Xinhua Bei Lu

→ To Fuzhou

Tianbao Banana Groves

Posts & Telecommunications Office

Shengli Lu

● **Bus Station**

● **Overseas Chinese Mansion/CTS**

Xinhua Dong Lu

Xinhua Xi Lu

Qingnian Lu

Zhongshan Park

Taiwan Lu

Yan'an Nan Lu

Xinhua Nan Lu

Jiulong River

Xiamen Lu

Nanshan Temple

Jiuhu Lychee Groves

Hundred-flower Village

Cotton Pavillion

N

operas, the productions are full of blood and thunder. So even if one doesn't understand the language there is plenty of action to sustain the visitor's interest.

The Talking and Singing-Song form is normally performed by one person accompanied by a string or maybe a wind instrument. The themes of the stories are simple and the acting minimal. During the New Year festivities there will probably be several groups performing at different ends of Zhongshan Park.

The Wooden Image Opera is usually performed by glove or sack puppets (see page 78). Chao Opera is not truly indigenous as it originated just across the border in Guangdong Province. Chao Opera is really a form of variety show combining acrobatics and dance with the singing and acting.

All forms of Zhangzhou opera are interesting to see. Immediately on arrival in your hotel enquire about what is playing. Performances are always popular so, except for the Talking and Singing-Song form, it is necessary to get tickets in advance.

Cotton Pictures Ask anyone in Zhangzhou what the town's most famous craft is, and the instant answer is cotton pictures. In 1964, the director of a cotton bedding factory, Mr Huang Jiasheng, tumbled on the idea of making pictures from the waste cotton. The craft has gone from strength to strength and has won numerous national prizes. One sees the pictures in public buildings all over China. They are also popular abroad, so much so that Mr Huang and his factory have set up a joint venture with an American organization, the latter advising on designs that will apppeal to their home market. The paintings, (collages must be more apposite) are normally traditional compositions — a pair of cranes perched on a pine branch (probably of real wood), or an orange sun about to set behind mountains, painted onto a silk background. It is well worth visiting the factory, **Zhangzhou Arts and Crafts Company**, at 35 Shengli Lu (tel. 3053) to watch these delicate pictures being put together. There is a shop which sells other crafts made in Zhangzhou as well as their own products.

Babao Ink Paste This red seal ink was first made in Zhangzhou by a man named Wei in 1673. It is made from musk, pearl, coral agate and four other ingredients, hence its name, 'eight-treasure' seal paste. Rather like a great chef refusing to disclose the recipe of his most successful dish, the makers of Babao paste have guarded the secret of their eight ingredients for 300 years. The colour of the paste is brilliant red and looks stunning in its little porcelain or wooden containers. It is much sought after by calligraphers as it is smooth, neither fades nor freezes in winter, nor dries up or becomes mouldy. Nor does the oil ever seep out. Dr Sun Yat-sen said it was even more precious than pearl. The Babao Ink Paste Factory is at 242 Qingnian Lu.

Pian Zi Huang This is a traditional medicine made from a secret formula created by an imperial physician of the Ming court. The physician retired to Zhangzhou to become a monk, bringing his secret with him. The medicine was then produced at the Pushan Monastery for generation upon generation, the secret always remaining in the hands of the abbot. After 1949 the abbot became a lay person and opened the Xinyuan Tea Shop where he marketed the potion under the Monk brand. In 1956 the government established the Zhangzhou Drug Factory to produce the medicine. It is made from a mixture of musk, snake's gall and other rare ingredients and is claimed to be good for a wide range of ailments from bullet wounds to chronic hepatitis.

Sights in Zhangzhou

Nanshan Temple

Nanshan Temple has an interesting story. Following a feud with the Prime Minister, a Song-Dynasty prince's tutor by the name of Chen Yong became disenchanted with court life. He decided to settle in Zhangzhou and there he built his new home in the palace style to which he had become accustomed (Song-Dynasty tutors evidently being better paid than their modern counterparts!). Unfortunately for Chen, news of his grandiose building reached court. To build above one's station (he was a mandarin of the third class, yet he had built the house of a first-class one) was then a crime which carried the death penalty for one's whole family. So a scheme had to be thought of quickly. Luckily for Chen Yong, he had a resourceful daughter who suggested that their new home should be converted into a monastery. History does not relate whether Chen Yong then became a monk or whether he joined his daughter (who indeed became a nun) and lived in the charming house at the back of the compound.

This is a well patronized temple. A monk stands in charge of a photograph stall, where one can have one's picture taken in front of Nanshan in tie and hat. The Main Hall is a fine building, supported by massive granite pillars, with a double hipped roof and a front wall of carved panels. Inside under a painted ceiling sit three large Buddhas with the Goddess of Mercy behind. And behind the Main Hall stands the Scripture Hall in which sits a Buddha image of white jade; weighing some 2,000 kilograms (4,410 pounds). It was brought here from Burma by Abbot Miaolian during the Qing Dynasty. You then come to Tutor Chen Yong's Memorial Hall, his daughter's grave and her house. Then there is a stone Buddha pavilion which houses an enormous image standing on lotus leaves cast in a single piece of stone-coloured bronze. Originally the sculpture was to be of Chen himself, but when he got into trouble over building the palace he quickly had it changed into a Buddha image.

On one side of the halls, amongst the monks' living quarters, is an excellent vegetarian restaurant (see page 90) run by the monks, of whom there are some 20 in residence and several nuns too. The beancurd they serve is made in the monastery — one sometimes sees a nun sitting on the steps kneading the curd.

Zhongshan Park

This is a pleasant park right in the middle of the city, beside the old market street, a short walk from the Overseas Chinese Hotel. Each spring during the Lantern Festival the competition for the city's best lantern is held here. Lanterns of every imaginable shape and size hang all over the park. Some are traditional in theme, such as a golden dragon which slowly revolves above a lantern hanging below; others are highly elaborate like the vast lotus-flower lantern set on the ground, which opens every few minutes and, from its centre, arises a Song-Dynasty princess. Many of the lanterns are advertisements for the businesses that created them. A typical one might be divided into four compartments, each one filled with models of that particular firm's goods. The lantern exhibition attracts huge crowds which in turn also attract the storytellers and magicians (the 'Talking and Singing-Song' groups), so the park becomes one huge opera theatre. At night with all the lanterns alight the park is spectacular, and of course the adjoining restaurant alley (see page 90) does a roaring trade. This is an outstanding time to visit Zhangzhou.

Sights outside Zhangzhou

Hundred-flower Village (Baihua Cun)

South of the Nanshan Temple and about seven kilometres (4.5 miles) from the city is the Hundred-flower Village. One leaves the main road and turns into the village which, at this stage, is simply a cart track flanked by neat, pot-filled gardens. At the end of the track is a sort of botanical garden. There is a story behind this 100-*mu* (6.67 hectares or 16.48 acres) garden and the surrounding village: during the Ming Dynasty a certain government official named Zhu Maolin, through bad management, contrived to lose a large amount of imperial silver, and escaped to Baihua to avoid the consequences. In a dream he was told

to plant a huge garden. Whether fact or fable, today the garden is well stocked and specializes in *bonsai*; it has several 200-year-old banyan *bonsais*. In the middle of the garden is a teahouse which, in the lychee season, attracts visitors from all over Southeast Asia. (The lychee groves themselves are but a few kilometres to the east of Baihua.) On the roof of the teahouse is a fine collection of cactus plants.

On the right as one walks out of the garden — there is only one gate — is the Ancestral Hall of the Zhu family. Today this charming Ming building is used as a barn. Strolling on up the hill it is possible to enter any of the roadside houses with their small but immaculate gardens. Their occupants seem quite happy to have their plants admired and happier still for them to be bought. The village claims to export 10,000 *bonsais* every year.

Cotton Pavilion (Mumian Ting)

South of the Hundred-flower Village and the lychee groves (see below) is the Cotton Pavilion. It was on this site that, during the last days of the Southern Song Dynasty, the Prime Minister Jia Sidao was beheaded by a junior military officer called Zheng Huchen. Jia Sidao is said to have been a ruthless and arbitrary politician whose sister was married to one of the imperial princes: he used this connection to further his own ends. Jia had plotted successfully against Zheng's father and engineered for Zheng himself to be exiled. However, the year 1275 saw Jia's downfall following the loss of an important battle against the Mongols for which he was held responsible.

Zheng in the meantime had been reinstated and vowed revenge, and the site of Jia's execution is now marked by a small Buddhist temple. It was built immediately after the execution, probably as an act of atonement by Zheng. It is looked after by the Cotton Society and is filled with small images. The worshipper makes a wish of his favourite image: if the wish is granted, he puts a jacket on the image. Many of them are covered in layer upon layer of cloth. A stone tablet relates the story of Jia and explains that he was executed in the cause of justice.

Lychee Groves

A few kilometres from Baihua on Fenghuang Shan are the Jiuhu lychee groves spreading over 1,000 hectares (2,472 acres). There is a good vantage point on the right of the main road which involves a brief climb; then suddenly for as far as the eye can see, the hills are covered with these majestic trees. To the south is a string of nine man-made

irrigation lakes. In March, the trees are covered in white blossom; by May the crowns of the trees have a reddish glow, made by the fronds of fruit beginning to form, which are then harvested in July. Lychee trees are short-lived and reach their fruit-bearing height at the age of only 20. By some curious quirk of nature every alternate year produces a bumper harvest. The groves contain 15 varieties of lychee of which five are considered to be superior. Delicious lychee wine can be brewed from any variety.

Banana Groves

There are 8,000 hectares (31 square miles) of banana groves west of Zhangzhou around the town of Tianbao. Bananas have been grown in the region for over 700 years: there are references to the delicious bananas of Zhangzhou in works by the Song-Dynasty poet Wang Anshi. Visiting a banana grove is fascinating as there is a continual cycle of growth and each plant will produce several new shoots which are then transplanted. Off some plants hang huge red seed pods, from others the embryo fronds of bananas. A plant has only one harvest, and the sapling produced in May produces the best crop. Throughout the groves you can see people hoeing, scattering fertilizer (both chemical and human is used), and strong young men, a pole slung across the shoulder supporting two baskets piled with young plants about to be transplanted. Harvest time is from July to October, but because of the continuing growth cycle, there are always some bananas available. The main varieties are grown, including the local Daiwan, which is small and sweet, and an Indian species first imported some 500 years ago. When the fruit has been harvested, slightly green, it is put in a smoke house for about three days, depending on the humidity. This is to extract excess water, acidity and stringiness, while incense is used as a flavour-enhancer. Along the road adjacent to the grove, large hands of unsmoked green bananas are for sale (many people have their own smokeries at home). An Institute of Development and Research in Zhangzhou is looking into ways of preserving the freshness of the banana for export. At present they distribute throughout China and export to Japan, but are looking to widen their market.

The market in Tianbao is well worth a visit: apart from foodstuffs there is a good selection of baskets and straw hats for sale — note the fetching bamboo hats with the leaves plaited from the crown. A popular stall is that of the starfish vendor. Dried starfish are popped into a pot with water and pork, and then drunk as soup, a brew considered an excellent remedy for stomach and headaches.

The Narcissus Area

To reach the narcissus growing area one must travel north, cross the Jiulong River and head east to the village of Xintang. The cultivated areas are only of interest to the visitor in early spring around Chinese New Year; then there are field upon field of narcissi on the point of bursting into bloom. Most are sold with bulb and flower intact, though some go to market as cut flowers. Narcissus cultivation has thrived in Fujian for at least 500 years and is the subject of much folklore. A version of one favourite fairytale follows.

A young man named Jing Zhan and his wife Bai Ye lived by the side of a lake in a rich and fertile land. One night there was a dreadful storm and in the morning the lake was totally covered by a round hill. With the source of water gone, the crops died and the land became barren. Jing Zhan had a dream in which he was instructed to travel to the 99th peak in the west where he should cut open the White Cloud mountain range and direct the water back to his area. He left home, but when winter came and neither he nor the water had returned, Bai Ye followed his footsteps. She found him weak and exhausted, and so took over his task. Eventually the water gushed from the rock, overcoming them with its force and volume. Some concerned villagers went in search of them, and, on reaching the White Cloud Mountains, sighted Jing Zhan and Bai Ye at the top of the peak. They turned, smiled and were lifted into the sky on a cloud. Moments later two glittering objects dropped down to earth and were immediately transformed into delicate flowers full of fragrance. The flowers were brought back to the village and at the end of spring they withered and were forgotten. However, to everyone's surprise, the following spring they sprouted up stronger than ever — Jing Zhan and Bai Ye had given their lives for water and had been reincarnated as narcissus flowers, which need only water to grow. The double flowered narcissus was named Bai Ye and the single variety Jing Zhan.

The Chinese narcissus is the same plant propagated from a bulb on a three-year cycle that is well known in the West, but in China the bulb, rather than being buried under soil, is grown in a bowl of water only accompanied by a few elegant stones. The bulb will have been sculpted, so it twists and turns like an old root. This treatment causes the bulb to produce many flowers and a little short foliage — an effect worthy of the plant's name in Chinese, 'water fairy'.

Dongshan Island

Dongshan Island, lying 120 kilometres (75 miles) southeast of Zhangzhou, is the province's second largest island. Its population of

150,000 is made up predominantly of fishermen whose regular catches include prawns, squids, anchovies, sardines and oysters in abundance.

Stone City of Dongshan In 1387 a stone city wall with a circumference of one kilometre (0.6 mile) was built with the intent of protecting the island, and of course the coast of Fujian Province as well, from Japanese pirates.

Military Temple (Wu Miao) This was built in 1389 to commemorate those killed fighting the Japanese pirates. The Prince Pavilion is of great architectural interest. This pavilion, which rests on stone pillars, is built on a site exposed to constant wind and even typhoons in the summer months — all of which it has survived. As is the case with many of Fujian's ancient buildings, the secret apparently lies in its complicated cross-beamed roof structure.

The Drive from Zhangzhou to Quanzhou

The distance from Zhangzhou to Quanzhou is 140 kilometres (87 miles). Some 14 kilometres (eight miles) out of Zhangzhou is a most bizarre building which turns out to be a Catholic church. Set back from the road on the far side of a lake is this two-storey square white folly, with a roof surmounted by two cupolas, two arches and a spire topped by a cross. No one seems to know when it was built or by whom, but services are held there once a month. With the mountains behind and the lake in front reflecting the church, the whole is a remarkable sight.

Wherever one drives in the Fujian countryside there is much to please and fascinate the eye. This particular stretch of road passes through undulating terrain; on either side of the predominantly tree-lined road are neat compartments of rice paddies and also fields of wheat and of different vegetables. The fields are punctuated by small hamlets, the houses all traditional in style with either hipped or vaulted ends to their roofs. With the influx of money from overseas Chinese to help their mainland relatives, a tremendous number of new houses are being built, almost all in the traditional style. Beside most villages is usually a duck pond, although it is also quite normal to see a duck minder walking his herd along the road to a nearby stream, swishing a long cane to keep his charges in order. On damp days the traditional straw raincoat is a frequent sight — one that seems to come straight out of a scene by one of the 'China coast' artists of the 19th century. Along this route are also many fine trees — the ones with extraordinary twisted grey bark and tops like paint brushes are known locally as 'horses tails'.

Xiamen

Xiamen, Fujian's second largest city, is situated in the southeast of the province. The city is actually a granite island with a total area of 124 square kilometres (48 square miles), lying in a deep bay protected from the full force of the South China Sea by a varied coastline which twists and curls and is punctuated with small islands. This strange formation has stimulated the growth of Xiamen as a port, for the islands have served both as breakwaters and a kind of sieve, preventing the silting problems which affected Quanzhou. Today Xiamen is connected to the mainland by a 2.2-kilometre (1.4-mile) causeway for both road and rail (at the time of writing a bridge was under construction). A geological fault runs from west to east dividing the island into a lower northern section, where the average height above sea level is around 150 metres (492 feet), and a southern section with strange rock formations, the highest of which (Cloud Top Rock) reaches 300 metres (980 feet). This spur of hills runs down to the sea at Tiger Head Hill and re-emerges as Dragon Head Hill on the other side of the strait on Gulangyu Island. Historically these two hills were called 'Dragon and Tiger on Guard'.

The recorded history of Xiamen begins during the Tang Dynasty (618–907), when it is said that the Xue clan from the Fuan district of Fujian and the Chen clan from the Putian district (north of Quanzhou) came to settle on the island. By the Song Dynasty (960–1279), an administrative office had been opened. During this period Xiamen became known for a special kind of grain which produced several ears on one stalk, and so the island was commonly called 'the isle of fine standing grain'. In 1387, a boundary wall was constructed and the city was fortified in an attempt to protect it from Japanese pirates. The year 1551 brought the first European traders, the Portuguese (they had made their first landing in the East at Macau during the previous year), who were keen to buy tea and silk in exchange for other textiles.

Though the defeat of the Ming Dynasty by the Manchu in 1644 was effected quickly in the north of China (the centre of the power base), it took the provinces further from Beijing some time to commit their allegiance. General Zheng Chenggong based his troops in fortified Xiamen to fight the invading Qing from 1650 on; in fact, Xiamen was the last Ming stronghold to survive. At the same time his troops were also fighting the Dutch, who had invaded Taiwan in 1623 and had created a flourishing colony. In 1659, he was finally defeated by the Qing and so moved his troops first to Quemoy, the offshore island opposite, then to the Pescadores and finally across the straits to Taiwan. His son continued to rule over the islands until 1683, when he was beaten by the superior Qing navy. Taiwan then officially became part of the Chinese Empire for the first time.

Xiamen began to expand quickly under the Ming Dynasty. Its sheltered port came into its own, too, when Quanzhou harbour began to be too silted up to be navigable. In 1842, after China's defeat in the first Opium War, the Treaty of Nanking stipulated that five ports be opened to foreign trade, and Xiamen, then known as 'Amoy', was one of these. (The others were Shanghai, Canton, Ningbo and Fuzhou.) During the years that followed, foreigners settled on Gulangyu Island, building consulates and imposing houses, many of which survive today.

Xiamen prospered until the Sino-Japanese War in 1937.–45, when the city, along with Fujian's other coastal areas, took the brunt of the Japanese aggression. Using occupied Taiwan as a jumping-off-point, the Japanese blockaded Xiamen. From time to time they occupied it to control the movement of their supplies into the Chinese hinterland and starve out the Chinese Nationalist headquarters in Chongqing.

Modern Xiamen continues to be a busy port, even boasting a newly constructed container terminal. In 1981, part of Xiamen was designated as China's third Special Economic Zone (see page 117) and, when Deng Xiaoping visited the city three years later, he decreed that the whole city enjoy that status.

The daily Fuzhou-Xiamen express train loops around inland for an overnight 603-kilometre (374-mile) journey scheduled to take 15 hours 38 minutes to Xiamen and 15 hours 52 minutes the other way. However, most visitors would probably prefer taking a bus — several daily buses take the much shorter 302-kilometre (197-mile) coastal route. Xiamen has an airport serving domestic routes and international flights from Hong Kong, Manila and Singapore. There is also a twice-weekly boat to and from Hong Kong.

Hotels in Xiamen

Xiamen Guesthouse
16 Huyuan Lu
tel. 22265
tlx. 93065, cable 6333

厦门宾馆
虎园路16号

71 double rooms, Rmb120; five suites, Rmb280–3,800 (the presidential suite boasts circular bath, sauna, jacuzzi, exercise bicycle, high glitz). Two Chinese restaurants, Western restaurant, coffee shop, banqueting facilities; swimming pool, sauna and massage parlour; conference room; disco. (Amex, Diners Club, MasterCard, Visa, Federal)

A joint venture with a Hong Kong corporation, this hotel opened in August 1986. It offers comfortable rooms, good food

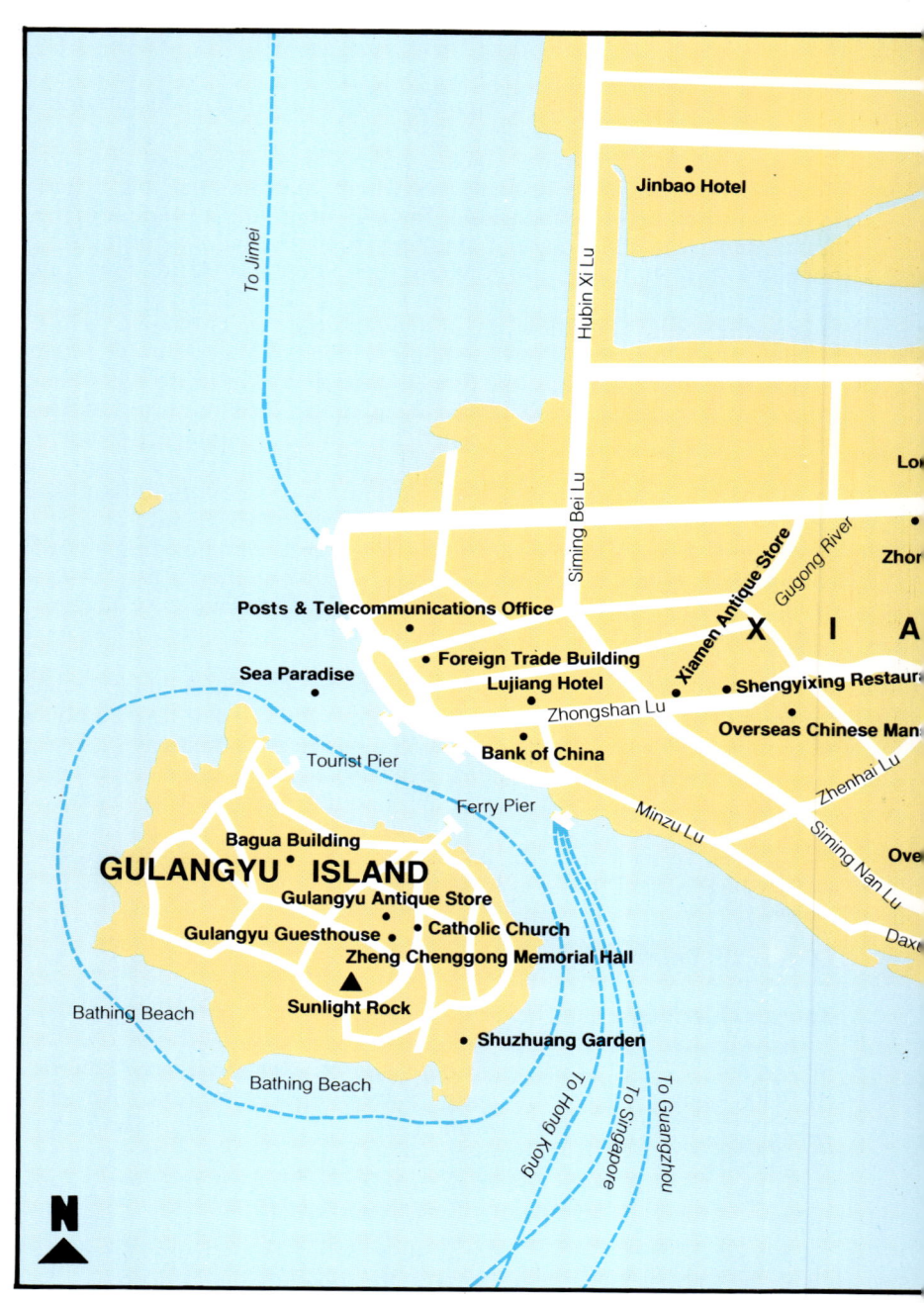

Jinbao Hotel

To Jimei

Hubin Xi Lu

Siming Bei Lu

Xiamen Antique Store

Gugong River

Lo·

Zhor·

X I A

Posts & Telecommunications Office

Sea Paradise

Foreign Trade Building

Lujiang Hotel

Shengyixing Restaur·

Zhongshan Lu

Overseas Chinese Man·

Tourist Pier

Bank of China

Zhenhai Lu

Ferry Pier

Minzu Lu

Siming Nan Lu

Ove·

Bagua Building

GULANGYU · ISLAND

Gulangyu Antique Store

Gulangyu Guesthouse · Catholic Church

Zheng Chenggong Memorial Hall

Daxe·

Sunlight Rock

Bathing Beach

Shuzhuang Garden

Bathing Beach

To Hong Kong

To Singapore

To Guangzhou

N

Mandarin Hotel

Hubin Zhong Lu

Hubin Nan Lu

To Jimei →

Bus Station

Xiahe Lu

Hotel

Railway Station

Wenyuan Lu

E   N

Xiamen Guesthouse

hite Egret Hotel

ese Museum

Nanputuo Temple

Xiamen University

Huli Shan Fortress

Bathing Beach

Xiamen

and helpful service from its charming staff. Its conference room, reputedly highly popular with the Japanese, is a surprise: lavishly furnished down to the gold Victorian-style telephones and decorated with pictures of English hunting scenes on the walls, it has adjacent to it a 'secretary's room' equipped with a two-way mirror looked in on from the games (mahjong) room next door!

Mandarin Hotel (Yuehua Jiudian)
Foreign Merchants
Residence Zone,
Huli
tel. 43333
tlx. 93028
fax. 41431

悦华酒店
湖里外商住宅区

74 double rooms, Rmb120−50; nine suites, Rmb290−360; 22 villas sleeping five to six people and including kitchen, dining and sitting rooms, Rmb450−500. Chinese and Western restaurants, banqueting facilities; swimming pool, tennis courts, games room; disco; conference rooms. (Amex, Diners Club, MasterCard, Visa)

Located out of the town centre, this is a joint-venture hotel with Hong Kong interests. The rooms are pleasantly furnished and the public areas have equally restrained decor with pale marble and bleached wood fittings. The banquets served here are excellent; the speciality — shark's fin and cucumber soup — is particularly delicious. The hotel also caters for businessmen spending several months in the SEZ who may bring their families to live in the self-contained villas in the grounds.

Lujiang Hotel
54 Lujiang Dao
tel. 22922, 24622
tlx. 93024, cable 1230

鹭江大厦
鹭江道54号

128 rooms, single (Rmb65), double (Rmb100) and 13 suites (Rmb130). Chinese and Western restaurants, coffee shop, banquet rooms; conference rooms; disco. (Amex)

Another Hong Kong joint venture, this attractively furnished hotel is well located on the seafront just opposite the ferry pier to Gulangyu Island. The bedroom walls are a little thin so take care to have one as far as possible from the disco.

Jinbao Hotel
Xingang Lu, Dongdu
tel. 26888
tlx. 93034

金宝饭店
东渡新港路

66 double rooms (Rmb90), 4 suites (Rmb180); Chinese and Western restaurants, banquet rooms, coffee shop; tennis courts; disco. (Diners Club, MasterCard, Visa)

This small and pleasant hotel opened about two years ago.

Singapore Hotel
113—21 Xi'an Lu
tel. 26668
tlx. 93069

新加坡饭店
西安路113-21号

10 single, Rmb48—70; 38 double rooms, Rmb64—90; 10 suites, Rmb80—120. Chinese restaurant, coffee shop; conference rooms; disco. (Amex, Diners Club, Visa)

Opened in 1986, this modest hotel provides medium-priced accommodation and standard facilities.

Overseas Chinese Hotel (Huaqiao Dasha)
70—4 Xinhua Lu
tel. 25602, 25701
tlx. 93029
fax. 31862

华侨大厦
新华路70－4号

242 double, Rmb52—70; 14 suites, Rmb120. Chinese and Western restaurants, coffee shop, banquet rooms; conference and business centre; disco

This hotel was in the process of renovation in mid-1987, but first signs are that management and maintenance still fall short of acceptable standards. It is hard to believe that the vast expanse of black marble and leather used in the public areas, which were the first part to be refurbished, are an improvement on the original interiors.

Sea Paradise (Haishang Leyuan)
'Egret' Passenger Ship
tel. 22506, cable 2867

海上乐园
客轮鹭江号

400 berths, single rooms (Rmb15); double rooms (Rmb30—70). Chinese restaurant, cafeteria; sundeck, video room; mahjong and other gambling facilities

This ship was built in Italy in 1968 and came to Xiamen in 1984. Sometimes it does the run to Hong Kong; otherwise it is permanently moored here and serves as a sort of scruffy floating casino.

View of Gulangyu Island and, across the harbour, the city of Xiamen, seen from Sunlight Rock. The cupola of the Eight Diagrams Building is clearly visible to the northwest.

Gulangyu Guesthouse
25 Huangyan Lu
Gulangyu
tel. 22052

鼓浪屿宾馆
鼓浪屿晃岩路25号

40 standard double with bathroom, Rmb47;
dormitory Rmb10 each bed

This complex of five turn-of-the-century grey
stone houses set in a beautiful garden was a
private residence (the former owner's
grandson is the deputy governor of Fujian). It
is now a hotel run by the provincial government and offers limited accommodation to
visitors. For a detailed description of this
interesting hotel see page 122.

**Seaview Garden
Hotel**
Gulangyu
tel. 26958, 26959

观海园
鼓浪屿

100 rooms in eight buildings, standard double
(Rmb70−100) ; Chinese and Western
restaurants, banqueting facilities; swimming
pool, tennis courts; disco, ballroom

A resort-type hotel jointly developed by the
Tourism Bureau and the Bank of China and
geared to weekend visitors from Hong Kong,
the Seaview Garden provides a pleasant oasis
on a car-free island. The management has
renovated a group of old European-style
houses and furnished them quite lavishly.
Some of them are close to the sea and the
hotel has its own beach, which is well kept.

Restaurants in Xiamen

**Shengyixing
Restaurant**
313 Zhongshan Lu
tel. 25964

生意兴小炒店
中山路313号

This restaurant, known locally by its street
number, is the most famous of the several
flourishing private restaurants in the
Zhongshan Lu area and is run by the Lin
family, who live upstairs. The front is open to
the street, and you can sit at one of the two
tables there and observe the street life. There
are more tables in the back. The restaurant is
is noted for its seafood dishes.

Morning Sun
325 Zhongshan Lu
tel. 24876

朝阳饮食店
中山路325号

This is a large restaurant, with a smart
upstairs dining room, which serves Fujianese
cuisine. It is essential to book.

Vegetarian Food Restaurant of Nanputuo Temple
Nanputuo Temple
tel. 22908

南普陀寺素菜馆
南普陀寺

This was once an outstanding restaurant, but overseas Chinese money has financed a new building, and outside chefs have been hired to cope with demand, so the monks and nuns no longer cook. You have to book a table in advance. Dinner is at 6 pm, when the dishes — the same for every table — are produced in rapid succession. Individual orders are taken only at lunch.

The atmosphere has suffered, and so has the food. Some beancurd dishes are still good, however; particularly good is beancurd stuffed with diced mushrooms. A wonderful yam mound called 'fragrant mud with hidden treasures' is stuffed with mushrooms and bamboo shoots. 'Half moon sunk into the river' is a mushroom and beancurd mound in soup. Open 11 am−1 pm and 6−8 pm.

Arts and Crafts in Xiamen

The one craft indigenous to Xiamen is lacquer thread sculpting. A specially prepared lacquer paste is rolled into a thin thread, then applied to a wooden, porcelain or lacquer object. Many modern religious artefacts are decorated using this technique, and it is highly sought after in Southeast Asia. In Dehua County, north of Xiamen, local artisans specialize in a fine white or rather milky coloured porcelain to make figurines, small pots and other domestic items. This Dehua ware is sold in the antique stores and in the better hotel shops and, although new, is quite expensive.

Visitors will also find other artefacts, such as silk figures, normally of sinuous court ladies in Tang-Dynasty dress, and clay figurines, including a fine line in Father Christmases which are also quite appealing. These models are always brightly coloured. A visit to the Arts and Crafts Service Department at 143 Zhongshan Lu will show examples of all these crafts as well as other artefacts produced in Fujian Province.

Shopping in Xiamen

There are two good antique shops in Xiamen (see Useful Addresses, page 136). The walls of the one in Xiamen are covered in glass cases which in turn are filled with porcelain of every shape and value. There are some large pieces of porcelain and a few items of furniture on sale, too. Purchased items can be shipped anywhere in the world. Even if one is not an avid collector this is a lovely shop to visit. The other antique shop is on Gulangyu, just below the Sunlight Rock; it also has interesting stock. Otherwise shopping is limited to the department stores or the hotel shops. However, the Xiamen Friendship Store is sparsely stocked and rather disappointing. Visitors are told that Xiamen is a centre of basket making and bamboo furniture — it's impossible to find any in the local shops.

Sights in Xiamen

Huli Shan Fortress

On the south coast of Xiamen island, protecting the entrance to the port from a strategic hilltop, is the Huli Shan Fortress, built in 1823 during the lead-up to the Opium Wars.

The fort consists of sturdy exterior walls and a series of trenches with underground living quarters inside. It was in turn occupied by the British, the Qing and the Nationalists, and served as a strategic naval defence base against the nearby island of Quemoy, which remains to this day in Nationalist hands. The Chinese Navy finally moved out of the fort in 1984 leaving it for tourists to enjoy.

On the semi-circular stone parapet a rusty cannon stands guard, pointing out over the estuary and beyond to a sea dotted with little islands and fishing junks, their sails billowing in the breeze. The shore line just below the fort is scattered with tarantula-like nets: the place is obviously a fisherman's paradise. To the left of the cannon is a powerful telescope trained on Quemoy, and readers of Chinese can make out the characters engraved in rock of Dr Sun Yat-sen's famous phrase: 'people's democracy, people's rights, people's livelihood'.

Xiamen University

Just west of Huli Shan Fortress is Xiamen University. This was Fujian's first university and was founded, built and endowed by Tan Kah Kee (see page 128) in 1919. It has a pleasant 100-hectare (247-acre) campus overlooking the sea. The main buildings are a mixture of east and west, solid stone structures with porticoes and Doric columns, topped by tiered Chinese roofs. Today there are some 5–6,000 students at the university and it is regarded as one of China's prime centres of learning, specializing in the sciences. For the visitor there are three interesting sights on the campus.

Memorial of Lu Xun   On the second floor of the Jimei Building (right in the centre of the campus) is a memorial hall dedicated to Lu Xun. This famed Chinese writer, philosopher and revolutionary lived and taught at Xiamen University from April 1926 to January 1927. The memorial comprises five rooms, four of which contain photographs of his revolutionary activities in Xiamen, as well as parts of his original manuscripts. (One article he wrote numbers some 200,000 words.) The fifth is a simple living room, probably still much as he left it: a desk with ink-stand, seal box, and alarm clock on a book shelf to its left. It was here that he wrote his treatise *The History of Chinese Fiction*.

   General Zheng Chenggong Drill Ground   Just a few sections of wall remain of the general's drill ground. But with a little imagination one can turn the clock back three and a half centuries from today's vast open playing field to the enormous concourse with Zheng's grotesquely clad soldiers in mass assembly. The modern Qunxian Hall stands on the site of the general's military drill pavilion.

   It is said that this area of the university was one of Lu Xun's favourite spots for walks and contemplation. Far from being moved by the beauty of the environment or by any joyful association, he was apparently sorry to recall that Xiamen had been the last Ming stronghold lost to the Manchus.

   The Museum of Anthropology   This is a charming, small museum well worth a visit. Its origins date back to 1926 when Lu Xun worked on setting up an exhibition of archaeological relics. Lin Huixiang, Professor of Anthropology, added to it to create an excellent collection and in 1934 began plans for a permanent museum site. The Sino-Japanese War in 1937 forced him to ship all his treasures to safety in Southeast Asia. In 1951, the collection was returned to Xiamen and was given to the university; the museum was finally opened in 1953.

   The building itself is more like a private house than a museum. The exhibition rooms, some of which even have small fireplaces, lead off a central passage. The exhibits show the evolution of man, and there is some nice porcelain. Halfway along the corridor on the right through one of the rooms is a door to the garden where there is a collection of Islamic tombs.

Nanputuo Temple

From the museum it is a gentle ten-minute walk to the Nanputuo Temple. This Buddhist temple was originally built during the Tang.

   The temple layout conforms to the Chinese Buddhist tradition. First one passes through the Hall of the Heavenly King which houses a statue of Maitreya Buddha, the Smiling Buddha, sitting cross-legged and guarded by four attendants, and one of Wei Tuo, who holds a staff which points to the ground. (This traditionally meant that the temple was rich and could afford to accommodate visitors.) One then crosses a large courtyard which has a bell and drum tower. At the far end stands the Main Hall. Unlike most main halls, this is not open to visitors. Inside are three statues of the Buddha. Behind the hall is a most pleasing building, the octagonal Great Mercy Hall (rebuilt in 1928). It is a small, well-proportioned hall with a three-tiered roof, topped by a little pagoda, and it sits jauntily up on a dais. Inside the goddess Guangyin is poised cross-legged on a lotus cushion.

Behind the octagonal hall is the library, a rather colourless structure. The drabness belies the library's contents — several tons of Buddhist and Chinese literature; priceless wood and ivory carvings, jade statues and other antiquities. Sadly, it is rarely open.

To the rear are stone steps, some carved into the rock of the hillside, which branch out in many directions leading to a number of stone carvings. One of the nearest, almost directly behind the library, is a vast, red-painted carving of the Chinese character for 'Buddha'. It was 'written' by a monk in 1869 (Qing Dynasty). In front of the bold character stands a little altar, and a monk sells joss sticks to worshippers. The Nanputuo Temple has many overseas benefactors and so has embarked on quite an ambitious building programme. The vegetarian restaurant here (see page 113), which used to offer one of China's finest gastronomic experiences, has recently moved into a purpose-built complex and the food is now unremarkable at best.

Five Old Men Peaks

Towering above the Nanputuo Temple are the Five Old Men Peaks. From a distance they resemble five old men looking out to sea, welcoming home compatriots. The hillside is covered with both acacia and flame of the forest (phoenix) trees. For the less hurried traveller with a taste for tranquil countryside, the slopes of the Five Old Men Peak offer beautiful walks and good sites for lazy picnics as well as visits to scenic spots such as the Lotus Flower Cave.

Overseas Chinese Museum

At the foot of Five Old Men Peak stands the Overseas Chinese Museum, which was built in 1956 by Tan Kah Kee (see page 128) and other overseas donors. Both the building and the garden are in the fine traditional Chinese style. The story of emigration is told through some 6,000 exhibits of the hard work, plights and successes of the overseas

Xiamen Special Economic Zone

Peter Fredenburg

A special economic zone is an area designated for intensive economic development, usually focusing on export-oriented or high-tech industries. Various incentives are offered to attract foreign investment and technological transfer. These include streamlining cumbersome foreign exchange procedures, import/export and labour regulations, eliminating or greatly reducing protective tariffs and instituting favourable tax and credit terms. Improved facilities for transport, communications, power-generating, manufacturing, housing and recreation are developed at State expense.

The Xiamen SEZ was declared in October 1981, originally covering only the 2.5-square-kilometre (one-square-mile) Huli Industrial District on the harbour-front midway between the city and the causeway linking Xiamen island to the mainland. The following year, construction commenced on 19 general-purpose factories and a residential quarter. The first foreign-invested enterprises began operating in 1984, the same year the SEZ was expanded to cover the whole of Xiamen and Gulangyu islands, and was redefined to include tourism and commerce as subsidiary activities to the mainstay of manufacturing for export.

By September 1986, nearly 140 projects utilizing US$240 million in foreign capital were in operation. Nearly three-quarters of the investors were from Hong Kong and Macau. Manufacturing absorbed over 40 percent of the investments, with tourist services taking another 20 percent.

The SEZ manufactures both light and heavy industrial goods — forklift trucks, tyres, chemicals — but these are generally not exported. Major exports include soft drinks and canned goods, agricultural by-products, televisions, bicycles, shoes and hats, handicrafts, and textiles. So far, growth in the total value of exports from the SEZ is reported to be respectable but not spectacular.

Imports have risen much faster and, while conceding that exports cannot keep pace with imports during the SEZ's tender years, government economists believe that too much hard currency has been squandered on non-essential consumer goods. Consequently, controls on imports of such items as electrical appliances are being enforced with renewed vigour.

A fish trap overlooked by the Huli Shan fort at Xiamen

*High jinks on (and off)
a beached fishing boat*

Chinese in their adopted countries, as well as of their undying loyalty and political support for the motherland (especially their hometowns), which includes substantial donations of money. The upstairs rooms are filled with objects used in daily life in their adopted homes.

Wan Shi Rocks and Botanical Gardens

On the east side of the city just north of the Overseas Chinese Museum are the Wan Shi Rocks (Ten-thousand Rocks). Visitors at the Xiamen Guesthouse will be only too aware of this remarkable geological phenomenon, for one of the gigantic rock grows up through the floor of the coffee shop.

Near the eastern end of the Ten-thousand Rocks are the **Botanical Gardens** covering 10,3 square kilometres (four square miles). Of chief interest is the Ten-thousand Rocks Reservoir with the Pine and Fir Garden on its eastern bank. Here in a small lotus pond grows the giant King Lotus (*Victoria amazonica*). This is a plant which was much loved by 19th-century botanical illustrators. It curls up at the edges of its vast leaves — up to two metres (2.2 yards) in diameter — which, several sources claim, can support weights of up to 75 kilograms (165 pounds).

Behind the fir section is the specimen building, where flower exhibitions are held and research work carried out. On its roof there is a fascinating collection of *bonsai* or miniature potted landscapes. As one has to pass through several offices to reach the roof, it is necessary to ask permission to visit this section. The most revered item here is a potted landscape containing a 300-year-old Chinese Elm. This section of the garden displays China's indigenous domestic flowers, the 'Ten Well-known Flowers' — the China rose, narcissus, peony, camellia and so on. All of these originated in China but are now to be found in gardens the world over in various forms.

For the cactus lover, there is a well-stocked section. Much research is being carried out into the medicinal properties of these plants. A species called *Lophophora williamsil coult* is of particular interest; it apparently contains a protein capable of killing cancer cells.

Perhaps the most interesting section of the garden, at the foot of the Purple Cloud Rock, is devoted to shade-loving plants — the bane of so many domestic gardeners' lives. In traditional Chinese style, the landscape has been incorporated into a man-made scheme. There is also a 'shade shed' in which particularly delicate mosses are being nurtured. The keen gardener or energetic walker could happily spend a whole day in this outstanding garden.

Zhongshan Park

North of the Xiamen Guesthouse lies this park dedicated to Dr Sun Yat-sen (the father of modern China); his statue stands at the eastern entrance. The park also contains a small but pleasant zoo. An outdoor stage as well as a indoor theatre have recently been created. The theatre has a unique form of natural air-conditioning: high pressure pumps are used to circulate cool air from an underground cave — much healthier than conventional air-conditioning and no doubt cheaper as well.

Sights outside Xiamen

Gulangyu

Gulangyu is an island to the southwest of Xiamen Island. Originally named Yuansha Zhou (Round Sand Islet), it became known as Gulangyu during the Ming Dynasty. The new name was derived from the following legend. Long ago, the islet was inhabited by two beautiful white egrets, whose home was a large cave on the southwest shore. Each day they would swoop and frolic around Sunlight Rock in the middle of the island. One day a lazy, hungry goshawk lay in wait and carried away the male. The female was heartbroken; day in and day out she perched on Sunlight Rock awaiting her mate's return. Finally one stormy night, she lay down and died. Feathers from her body were caught by the wind and floated down to sea. She was mourned by the seagulls who continually cried 'ow, ow' until eventually their cry was heard by the sea god. He moved the waves to lash into the cave which was once the egrets' home, making a sound like a beating drum. Gulang literally translates as 'drum wave'. The geography of this 1.71-square-kilometre (0.66-square-mile) island is dominated by the Sunlight Rock, the highest peak from the spur of the Dragon Head Hills which run under the water onto Xiamen Island.

The Xiamen-Gulangyu ferry runs every 15 minutes from a pier just opposite the Lujiang Hotel. The crossing takes about five minutes.

Gulangyu is famed for its musicians; in fact two of China's currently renowned violinists come from here. Visitors will notice that the booking office on the island pier is in the shape of a grand piano. It is said that at least one member of every Gulangyu family will play a musical instrument, the most popular being the violin. Wandering around the island in the afternoon or early summer evening, the visitor may catch strains of music, and on every Christmas Eve a carol service takes place — there are thriving Christian churches on the island.

To visit Gulangyu at a leisurely pace one must allow about four or five hours; there are no cars or vehicles of any kind on the island, and its natural beauty is inspiring. The island provides a fascinating mixture of Eastern and Western architecture. And there are numerous little teahouses and restaurants to stop in.

Catholic Church

On alighting from the ferry, take the road to the left along the seafront and then the first right up the hill. Passing a large red-brick house, formerly the British Consulate (at the height of Treaty-Port days Gulangyu was host to 13 or 14 consulates), one can either follow the road up the hill or take a short cut through the garden of the Yude Middle School (once the British School). The short cut brings you to the entrance of the Xiamen Aihua Hotel, built by the Catholic Church in 1986. From here the church is quite visible — a fine stone building, dating from 1882, set on Lujiao Lu. Inside, it is decorated in blue wash and has a grand vaulted ceiling faced with bamboo. Little gold stars are painted on the blue ceiling over the altar; a large painting of Jesus hangs behind. The nave is furnished with original teak pews, the kneelers now topped with red cushions; on each pew are several bamboo fans. The provincial government recently gave the church funds for restoration. This is the only Catholic church in the area (the one on Xiamen Island was demolished), and the local parishioners number some 200. Mass is celebrated every morning at 8.30.

Gulangyu Guesthouse

To get to the Gulangyu Guesthouse, continue along Lujiao Lu past the hospital, proceed on down into Huangyan Lu and just past the sports ground; to the left are the gates. For anyone interested in period building the guesthouse is well worth a visit. It is a collection of grey stone houses set in a lovely garden dotted with old banyan trees. The houses were built around the turn of the century for a local trader named Mr Huang. The main house would have been where Mr Huang lived and entertained, while the other family members would have inhabited the secondary houses. It still contains its original furniture and porcelain. One enters through a large portico into a panelled drawing room. On the far side of the room stands an original dresser. Next door is a billiard room, complete with billiard table, leading out onto a vast, serpentine marbled verandah. The white cane furniture looks to be the original, though it is doubtful that it could have survived in a semi-tropical climate. Perhaps the building's *pièce de*

résistence is its staircase, though it is by no means grand and is tucked
unobtrusively at the side of the building. It is made of white marble
complete with white marble dado and bannisters. In fact it is rather
delicate in comparison to the rest of the house. When the building was
restored by the provincial government (which manages the
guesthouse), the wall above the marble dado was papered with a
charming green flock bamboo pattern in the best Victorian *chinoiserie*
tradition. 'Foreign friends' and overseas Chinese can stay at the
guesthouse (see page 112), and for visitors who want a few days away
from honking horns and are interested in 19th-century architecture,
this is the place.

Sunlight Rock

Continue up the road and towering above is the 90-metre (295-foot)
Sunlight Rock. At the end of the first flight is a terrace leading to the
700-year-old **Lotus Flower Monastery** (Lianhua Si). This is in fact a
little temple set into the rocks so it is roofed by the rock. The
monastery is known locally as the Sunlight Monastery — not as one
would think because it is at the foot of Sunlight Rock but because it
faces east and fills with the first rays of the rising sun. On the north
side of the building is the Rising Sun Pavilion (Xuri Ting), a sort of
prayer hall, and on the south side is a tea-room. Continue the climb up
the steep stone steps between the temple and pavilion through the
stone arch called the Moon Cave Gate (Yuedong Men). This doorway
was built in 1661 as the gate to General Zheng Chenggong's fortress,
for it was here that he drilled his troops before sailing off to rout out
the Dutch from Taiwan. It is hard to imagine this rocky enclosed area
being a fortress but there are holes in the rock where the building's
beams were once secured. Today the visitor can have a photograph
taken wearing court robes to commemorate a visit to this historic spot.

Leaving the fortress, the steps continue up to what looks like a
cave but, on closer inspection, turns out to be two rocks forming a
hollow. Stop in the middle, look up, and on the roof are the characters
'Gu Bi Shu Dong', which translate into 'Ancient Avoid Heat Cave'.
Indeed, there is always a breeze flowing through this cave, so it is a
good place to pause, collect one's breath and prepare for the final
assault. The remainder of the climb, which is fairly steep, is up narrow
stone steps. It is advisable to visit Sunlight Rock in the early morning.
Not only will the climb be cooler but also less crowded: undoubtedly
some of the beauty of the climb is marred if getting to the top becomes
an exercise in elbow power. Nevertheless, even if the final climb has
been rather squashed, it is worth it. The view from the 'high platform

one hundred metres high' of the full grandeur of Gulangyu's European-style buildings — the pink, terracotta and yellow walls, the burnt orange roof tiles, the whole a patchwork of oranges and greens — and of the fine trees rising above the roofs, is marvellous. To the northwest the view is dominated by the grandiose cupola of the **Eight Diagrams Building** (Bagua Lou), which is soon to house a museum of Xiamen's history. It was originally a private villa built by an overseas Chinese merchant. Construction began in 1941 and all the materials were imported, but the owner ran out of money and the building was completed by the government after 1949. Bagua Lou served as a school until the Cultural Revolution, when it became an electronics factory.

Descend the narrow steps and follow the northern slope to Wanzai Pavilion where a perceptive message is carved on the rock, 'When the strength of your feet is exhausted, the hill will look more beautiful'. Passing through the pavilion one arrives at the relic of General Zheng's command platform, where, to the right, the rock-face is adorned with calligraphy dating from the Ming and Qing eras and some of which is said to be written in the style of General Zheng.

Zheng Chenggong Memorial Hall

Just below the command platform is General Zheng Chenggong's Memorial Hall. It was opened on 28 January 1962, the 300th anniversary of his victory over the Dutch in Taiwan. General Zheng's mother was Japanese and when he was seven years old he returned to Fujian. There is a theory that he chose the base of Sunlight Rock as his stronghold because the rock formation reminded him of Japan. The Memorial Hall is an impressive building with a magnificent central staircase which divides into two on the first landing. The ground-floor and first-floor rooms are filled with memorabilia of the general's life and campaigns: jade belts, his poems, shoes, pieces from his robes, silver coins which he had minted to defray military costs, his seals, maps of his battles, a stone mortar for preparing gunpowder. In the entrance hall are a life-size statue of General Zheng in armour and two huge canvasses of his battles with the Dutch, filled with gory detail.

Shuzhuang Garden

From the memorial hall follow the road down to the sea. Many Gulangyu roads are unmarked but, as the island is so small and the terrain is hilly, one can normally see any destination. Make for the Gang Zi Hou bathing beach on the south side of the island. On reaching the long sandy beach turn left, and on the right hugging the rock will be the entrance to the Shuzhuang Garden.

This was a private garden started in 1913 by Lin Shuzhuang (also known as Lin Erjia). His family originated in southern Fujian but had moved to Taiwan. In 1894, the Chinese were defeated by the Japanese in the Sino-Japanese War and lost Taiwan, so the Liu family came back to Gulangyu.

This garden of some four hectares (ten acres) is true to the Chinese tradition and full of little architectural tricks and puzzles. Again it is worth visiting early in the morning or late in the afternoon to avoid the crowds. Chinese gardens were designed for the elite literati: when they are crowded it is difficult to catch their subtle nuances.

Mr Lin's garden is supposed to be based on the same architectural style and composition as the Yihong Yuan belonging to Jia Baoyu in the famous novel *The Dream of the Red Chamber*. The garden is divided into two parts: Canghai Yuan (Sea Hide Garden) and Bushan Yuan (Hill Mending Garden). Throughout the garden there are named scenes, five in the Canghai Yuan and five in Bushan Yuan.

In Canghai Yuan one finds the Forty-four Bridge zigzagging its way out to sea. The story is that Mr Lin built this bridge in celebration of his 44th birthday and therefore intended it to have 44 turns ending up in the neighbouring garden of the Guanhai Villa which belonged to his cousin by marriage. However, modern technology interfered with his plan: the bridge would have had to cross a submerged telegraph cable and the Dutch firm involved would not allow it.

The Bushan Yuan is planted with abundant bougainvillaea (the flower of Xiamen) of all shades, as well as wisteria and jasmine. Altogether the Shuzhuang is a charming example of a Chinese garden that has used all the classical ingredients — water, rocks, the natural landscape and, of course, plants.

Other Sights Around Gulangyu

On the way back to the ferry a wander around Gulangyu's downtown area can be highly enjoyable. Turn right out of the Shuzhuang Garden and go up the hill back to the centre of the island. Many of the shops along the way sell beautifully made shell ornaments and other tourist trinkets. Practically every other shop is a seafood restaurant. Just north of the Gulangyu Tourist Hotel is a little enclosed square where you can sit outside and watch life go by. The Gulangyu Antique Shop at 71 Yongchun Lu is worth a visit as is the **Protestant Church**. The pastor is now 80 so he relies on visiting missionaries to take the services for him. His congregation is said to number about 500.

Another enjoyable way to see Gulangyu is to take the boat trip round the island: it lasts roughly an hour and costs Rmb1. The somewhat spartan but covered craft leaves from the Xiamen side just beside the regular ferry.

Jimei

Until 1955, Xiamen was cut off from the mainland and therefore from Jimei, a barren strip of land jutting into Xiamen Bay. The people of Xiamen relied on ferries to make the ten-kilometre (six-mile) crossing. Going downstream the journey took an hour, upstream perhaps an hour and a half. (These waters are fairly treacherous; in 1931, 189 passengers lost their lives when a ferry capsized.) Construction of a causeway began in 1953 and took two years to complete. There are two sections, one connecting Xiamen with Jimei and the second linking Jimei and Xinglin.

Jimei School Village There apears to be no early history of Jimei. During the Tang Dynasty it was inhabited by duck farmers. For a short period during late Ming times General Zheng Chenggong stationed his troops here. When he moved across to Xiamen, his subordinate, General Liu Guoxuan, remained with some troops and a fortress was built (a small section of the gate can still be seen today). Prosperity and national recognition came to the area from 1913 when Tan Kah Kee (see page 128) started on his philanthropic programme for free education in the surrounding neighbourhoods — from kindergartens, middle and upper schools to technical institutes of navigation, agriculture and commerce. The government took on the funding of the project in 1956 although Mr Tan remained involved.

The main buildings of this compound are huge and impressive, the architecture not unlike that of Xiamen University. They are lined up along the seafront, and at the end on the eastern tip of the land is a museum and Tan Kah Kee's tomb. The museum is housed in a charming two-storey building which Mr Tan used during his periodic visits to Jimei between 1912 and 1922. Part of the house as well as the schools were destroyed during Japanese occupation (in the Sino-Japanese War, 1937—45). In keeping with his character, the schools were restored first, his residence second. Tan Kah Kee lived here until death in 1961. The museum contains a fascinating photographic record of his life — in his office there are spectacles on the desk, letters, a fan, and a *chaise longue* all as they were when he was alive. The impression is of a humble man who enjoyed a simple life.

Walking from the house towards Mr Tan's tomb, one passes a huge ancestral hall built by Tan's family, construction of which began in

Tan Kah Kee

By his massive philanthropy and intense commitment to the cause of China's unification Tan Kah Kee (Chen Jiageng)* earned a place as one of China's best-loved sons. His life spanned several cycles of profound change. Born in 1874, he lived through the demise of the Manchu (Qing) Dynasty, Sun Yat-sen's emergence, the warlord period, the rise and fall of the Nationalist government and finally the establishment of the communist People's Republic.

Jimei, a village situated on an exposed peninsula just north of Xiamen island, was his birthplace. He was one of two sons; his father Tan Kee-Peck had a successful rice business in Singapore and so the boys were brought up by their mother. At the age of 17 Tan Kah Kee left home to join his father, eventually taking over from him and expanding the business by diversifying into pineapples and rubber.

Like many overseas Chinese, Tan Kah Kee had a deep-rooted love for his motherland. 'Think of the source of water when drinking,' he said, 'never forget the basic.' He was convinced that education was the key to modernizing China, and in 1913 he opened a primary school in Jimei; by 1916 he had added a secondary and a teacher's training college. This was followed in 1919 by Amoy University and in 1925 by the opening of a Marine and Navigating School. He endowed the schools fully and the university partially, for he was convinced that, by taking the lead in subsidizing education, other prominent overseas Chinese would follow suit. Sadly in this instance he was mistaken, and in later years he was forced to travel the world fund-raising.

Tan Kah Kee had four wives and 17 children but was not a 'family man'. In Singapore he spent most of his time living in a small underfurnished room in the Ee Ho Hean Club. He would rise around 5 am, exercise, have breakfast, then visit his various factories. He might lunch at one of his two residences, then go back to work and have dinner at his club, where he would discuss China, her problems, and how the powerful overseas community could best help.

In 1916 Tan Kah Kee applied for and was granted British citizenship, a fact which signified approval from the colonial authorities. However, this move was motivated by business: there was a shortage of merchant ships during the First World War, and he needed British citizenship to buy the two ships he required.

In the 1920s Tan became actively involved in Chinese politics. Power was divided between the warlords, Chiang Kai-shek and the Nationalists, and Mao Zedong and the communists, with the Japanese hovering around the coast (they had invaded Taiwan and Korea). In 1927, Tan, very worried by this situation, sent a telegram to Chiang urging him to cease fighting a civil war, and to make common cause with the communists to stop a Japanese invasion. As leader of the Hokkien Huay Kuan *bang*, a socio-political group, Tan was able to use his powerful position to help China. In 1937, on the outbreak of the Sino-Japanese

War, Tan had the Hokkien Huay Kuan organize the Singapore China Relief Fund which sent much needed resources to Chiang Kai-shek at the Nationalist headquarters, then in Chongqing. In 1938 a larger relief organization, called Southsea China Relief Fund, was formed, again under the Chairmanship of Tan Kah Kee. The SCRF also provided material support to the war effort.

Tan was, however, to be disillusioned. He himself witnessed, during a comfort mission to Chongqing, the corruption and profligate waste among the Nationalist Army. 'The frontline was tense in battle,' he commented, 'the backline was tense in pleasure-seeking.'

The non-partisan Tan had always said he wanted to visit the communist headquarters in Yan'an. This he did and in contrast was much impressed. He found Mao Zedong to be public-spirited and a loyal patriot. Furthermore he predicted that Mao and not the 'cunning, crafty dictator Chiang Kai-shek' would be 'China's saviour'.

Tan along with several other prominent anti-Japanese activists spent the years 1942−5 in Indonesia. Once back in Singapore Tan was again able to devote most of his energy to China's welfare, and also to the ending of the Chiang Kai-shek regime. By June 1948 Mao Zedong had taken Beijing and invited Tan to attend the People's Political Consultative Conference, an invitation he declined. But in May 1949 he travelled via Hong Kong to Beijing.

Tan spent ten months in China, became a member of the PPCC and announced his intention of settling in Jimei, his hometown. He returned briefly to Singapore to hand over his remaining businesses to his sons and, by May 1950, was back in Jimei. For the last 11 years of his life he was active, taking up overseas Chinese interests from within the motherland. As always, the welfare of his province was well to the fore. In 1954 he managed to persuade the central government to build a railway in Fujian. Naturally much of this time was also spent on the affairs of his beloved schools and university.

Tan Kah Kee died on 12 August 1961, aged 87. Although he was born into wealth and privilege, both of which he multiplied many fold, he was accorded a state funeral in Beijing by the communist authorities. He strove tirelessly for the cause of China's unity yet spent most of his life beyond her borders. He became an important voice in the international political forum yet spoke neither Mandarin nor English. All of these contradictions, however, were resolved in his unswerving, practical, munificent devotion to his motherland, and for this Tan Kah Kee will be remembered as the quintessential overseas Chinese.

* 'Tan Kah Kee' is a phonetic translation of the name in Chinese based on its pronunciation in the southern Fujian dialect, Hokkien. In Mandarin the name translates as 'Chen Jiageng'.

Vernacular Architecture in Fujian

Chinese vernacular architecture, varying markedly in style in its adaptation to geography, climate and the needs of daily life, has a history of some 6,000 years. Chengqi Lou (illustrated here) is a typical example of the circular communal dwelling of Hakka people in western Fujian. The Hakka were migrants, and the defensive style of this building — believed to be about 300 years old — is a telling reflection of the hostility that they often aroused in the settled inhabitants. The outer mud wall of Chengqi Lou surrounds an internal wooden structure of over 400 rooms, occupied by about 600–700 people. The upper-floor storage rooms and living quarters are arranged round a central communal space in which are the ancestral clan halls and kitchens. Important ceremonies such as weddings and funerals are held in this central ring. (*Photographs and information courtesy of David Lung, University of Hong Kong.*)

1961, the year of his death. The architectural style echoes that of his schools, with a European base and ornate Chinese roofs. At the far end of the garden stands a bronze statue, put there in 1983, the 70th anniversary of his first donation.

Turtle Garden (Aoyuan) and Tan Kah Kee's Tomb The Turtle Garden sits on a small island at the eastern point of Jimei. There are no trees here, and the wind whistles through; it is easy to understand why Jimei was uninhabited until the Tang Dynasty. There used to be a small monastery here called Ao Head Palace (*Ao* is the name of a legendary sea turtle which symbolizes peace and longevity), but it was destroyed by bombs during the Sino-Japanese War. In 1950, Mr Tan began to rebuild on the site and indeed designed his own tomb. To the right and left of the garden's entrance stands an excellent exhibition of the major events of China's history, illustrated both with drawings and photographs. Past the exhibition is an 11-storey monument to the liberation of Jimei. The 11 storeys represent eight years of resistance against the Japanese and three years' war of liberation. On the front are some characters written by Mao Zedong; in the rear is an inscription by Tan Kah Kee explaining the moument's purpose. Around the base of the monument and around the perimeter walls are carved tablets, some of animals, others of flowers, vegetables, agricultural scenes and characters from famous Chinese classics such as *The Dream of the Red Chamber*. Individually these carvings are sensitive and beautiful. However, as a whole its impact is more that of a powerful statement than a work of art. The body of the monument is of granite, the inlaid carvings of a stone known as *qingshi* which is quarried near Quanzhou. Much of the carving was done by people from Hui'an (see page 81).

The tomb itself is created in the shape of the mythical turtle after which the garden is named; the screen wall behind is decorated with carvings depicting Mr Tan's life. On the other side is a small pavilion for visitors to rest in. The complex took ten years to construct and was finished in 1960, a year before Tan Kah Kee's death.

Recommended Reading

Reading material in English on Fujian Province is scarce. This is strange because during the Middle Ages Quanzhou (Zaytun) was one of the world's busiest ports. And some 500 years later Fuzhou (Foochow) and Xiamen (Amoy) became Treaty Ports and from 1842 to 1949 were home to several generations of foreigners. However, colourful accounts of Zaytun appear in *Marco Polo: The Travels* (Penguin 1958), *The Mongol Mission* by Christopher Dawson (Sheed and Wand, 1935) and *Cathay and the Way Thither* by Henry Yule (Hakluyt Society, 1915). The last two tell the stories of three Franciscan missionaries, Peregrine of Castello (who in fact became Bishop of Zaytun), Andrew of Perugia and Odoric of Pordenone.

Of later expatriate experiences *China Trader* by A. H. Rasmussen (Constable, 1954), *Servant of the Dragon Throne* by Charles Drage (Peter Dawnay, 1966) and *The British in the Far East* by George Woodcock (Atheneum, New York 1969) are interesting accounts. In *China Races* by Austin Coates (Oxford University Press, 1983) there is an amusing chapter on horse racing in Foochow and Amoy during their Treaty-Port days.

On Fujian's two most celebrated heroes, Tan Kah Kee and Commissioner Lin, there are several publications from which to choose. A new biography entitled *Tan Kah-Kee, The Making of an Overseas Chinese Legend* by C. F. Yong (Oxford University Press, 1987) is informative if a little heavy-going. *Commissioner Lin and the Opium War* by Chang Hsin-Pao (Harvard University Press, 1964) and *The Opium War through Chinese Eyes* by Arthur Waley (Allen and Unwin, 1958) are both illuminating.

The history, the making, and some of the plays performed by the puppets of Fujian are described in *China's Puppets* by Roberta Helmer Stalberg (China Books, 1984). Michael Carter's *Crafts of China* (Aldus Books, 1977) provides background to some of the province's crafts. Today's artists are discussed by Joan Lebold Cohen in *The New Chinese Painting, 1949–1986* (Harry N. Abrams, 1987).

For those in search of help in understanding China as a whole, Brian Catchpole's *A Map History of Modern China* (Heinemann, 1978) helps clarify her complicated history from the Qing Dynasty to the present day. A broad and perceptive look at China's present economic, political and cultural scene is provided by Lynn Pan's *The New Chinese Revolution* (Hamish Hamilton, 1987).

Some of the above are no longer in print though most are available in good libraries and often can be found in second-hand bookshops.

Useful Addresses

Fuzhou

Antiques and Curios Store
Wuyi Lu
tel. 53702
福州文物商店　　五一路

Bank of China
300 Baiyiqi Lu
tel. 51775, 51206
tlx. 92109
Cable 51009
中国银行　　八一七路300号

CAAC (Civil Aviation Administration of China)
Wuyi Zhong Lu
tel. 51988
中国民航　　五一中路

China International Travel Service (CITS)
44 Dongda Lu
tel. 555496
中国国际旅行社　　东大路44号

China Travel Service (CTS)
Overseas Chinese Mansion
4 Wusi Lu
tel. 56304, 57603
tlx. 92123
Cable 8312
中国旅行社　　华侨大厦五四路4号

Foreign Languages Bookstore
122 Bayiqi Lu
tel. 550889
外文书店　　八一七路122号

Friendship Store
Bayiqi Lu
tel. 32106
友谊商店　　八一七路

Posts and Telecommunications Bureau
Posts and Telecommunications Building
tel. 31823
邮电管理局　　邮电大楼

Quanzhou

Bank of China
Jiuyi Lu
tel. 4693, 4618
Cable 6892
中国银行　　九一路

China International Travel Service (CITS)
Jiuyi Lu
tel. 2039
中国国际旅行社　　九一路

China Travel Service (CTS)
Overseas Chinese Mansion
tel. 2366, 2191
Cable 5132
中国旅行社　　华侨大厦

Civil Aviation Administration of China (CAAC)
Booking Office
Baiyuan
tel. 3410
中国民航售票处　　百源

Friendship Store
Zhongshan Nan Lu
tel. 2294
友谊商店　　中山南路

Posts and Telecommunications Office
Jiuyi Lu
tel. 4152
邮电管理局　　九一路

Zhangzhou

China People's Construction Bank
Shengli Lu
tel. 3496
中国人民建设银行　　胜利路

China Travel Service (CTS)
38 Yan'an Bei Lu
tel. 3882
Cable 4357
中国旅行社　　延安北路38号

Posts and Telecommunications Office
Shengli Lu
tel. 3914
邮电管理局　胜利路

Zhangzhou Railway Station
Nankeng
tel. 3585
漳州火车站　南坑

Xiamen

Antique Store
211 Zhongshan Lu
tel. 23363
厦门文物商店　中山路211号

Arts and Crafts Service Department
143 Zhongshan Lu
工艺美术门市部　中山路143号

Bank of China
Xiamen Branch
4−10 Zhongshan Lu
tel. 25870, 25286, 22483
tlx. 93012
Cable 6892
中国银行　中山路4-10号

China International Travel Service (CITS)
44 Zhongshan Lu
tel. 24286, 22721
Cable 3330
中国国际旅行社　中山路44号
Lujiang Hotel
tel. 25277
tlx. 93063
fax. 31832
中国国际旅行社　鹭江大厦

China Travel Service (CTS)
70−4 Xinhua Lu
tel. 25602, 25701
tlx. 93029
fax. 31862
中国旅行社　新华路70-4号

Foreign Trade Corporation of Xiamen SEZ
4th Floor, Foreign Trade Building
tel. 24612, 21489
tlx. 93011
Cable 6319
厦门经特区对外贸易公司
外贸大楼4楼

Friendship Store
122−4 Xinhua Lu
友谊商店　新华路122-4号

Gulangyu Antique Store
71 Yongchun Lu
Gulangyu
鼓浪屿文物商店　永春路71号

Hongkong and Shanghai Banking Corporation
Xinhua Lu Zhongduan
tel. 25690
tlx. 93016
fax. 31883
香港上海汇丰银行　新华路中段

International Airport
Enquiries
tel. 25902, 20630
厦门国际飞机场　讯问处

Overseas Chinese Bank
Xiamen Branch
Zhongshan Lu
tel. 22653
华侨银行　中山路

Overseas Chinese Store
7 Zhongshan Lu
tel. 24163
Cable 3676
华侨商店　中山路7号

Posts and Telecommunications Office
Xinhua Lu
tel. 22629
邮电管理局　新华路

Standard Chartered Bank
Room 403, Lujiang Hotel
tel. 22922, 24622
tlx. 93024
标准渣打(麦加利)银行
鹭江大厦403室

Travel Services to Fujian in Hong Kong

Hong Kong Dragon Airlines Ltd
19th Floor, Wheelock House
20 Pedder Street
Hong Kong
tel. 5–8105105
tlx. 80253
fax. 5–8100370
港龙航空公司 香港中环毕打街20号19楼

Hua Min Tourism Co. Ltd
2108–10 Wing On House
71 Des Voeux Road
Central
Hong Kong
tel. 5–244061, 5–8104118
tlx. 64597
fax. 5–8101863
华闽旅游有限公司
香港中环德辅道中永安集团大厦2108-10室

Chronology of Periods in Chinese History

Palaeolithic	c.600,000−7000 BC
Neolithic	c.7000−1600 BC
Shang	c.1600−1027 BC
Western Zhou	1027−771 BC
Eastern Zhou	770−256 BC
Spring and Autumn Annals	770−476 BC
Warring States	475−221 BC
Qin	221−207 BC
Western (Former) Han	206 BC−8 AD
Xin	9−24
Eastern (Later) Han	25−220
Three Kingdoms	220−265
Western Jin	265−316
Northern and Southern Dynasties	317−589
Sixteen Kingdoms	317−439
☐Former Zhao	304−329
☐Former Qin	351−383
☐Later Qin	384−417
Northern Wei	386−534
Western Wei	535−556
Northern Zhou	557−581
Sui	581−618
Tang	618−907
Five Dynasties	907−960
Northern Song	960−1127
Southern Song	1127−1279
Jin (Jurchen)	1115−1234
Yuan (Mongol)	1279−1368
Ming	1368−1644
Qing (Manchu)	1644−1911
Republic	1911−1949
People's Republic	1949−

A Guide to Pronouncing Chinese Names

The official system of romanization used in China, which the visitor will find on maps, road signs and city shopfronts, is known as *Pinyin*. It is now almost universally adopted by the Western media.

Non-Chinese may initially encounter some difficulty in pronouncing romanized Chinese words. In fact many of the sounds correspond to the usual pronunciation of the letters in English. The exceptions are:

Initials

c	is like the *ts* in 'i*ts*'
q	is like the *ch* in '*ch*eese'
x	has no English equivalent, and can best be described as a hissing consonant that lies somewhere between *sh* and *s*. The sound was rendered as *hs* under an earlier transcription system.
z	is like the *ds* in 'fa*ds*'
zh	is unaspirated, and sounds like the *j* in '*j*ug'

Finals

a	sounds like 'ah'
e	is pronounced as in 'h*er*'
i	is pronounced as in 'sk*i*' (written as *yi* when not preceded by an initial consonant). However, in *ci*, *chi*, *ri*, *shi*, *zi* and *zhi*, the sound represented by the *i* final is quite different and is similar to the *ir* in 'sir', but without much stressing of the *r* syllable.
o	sounds like the *aw* in 'l*aw*'
u	sounds like the *oo* in '*oo*ze'
ê	is pronounced as in 'g*e*t'
ü	is pronounced as the German *ü* (written as *yu* when not preceded by an initial consonant)

The last two finals are usually written simply as *e* and *u*.

Finals in Combination

When two or more finals are combined, such as in *hao*, *jiao* and *liu*, each letter retains its sound value as indicated in the list above, but note the following:

ai	is like the *ie* in 't*ie*'
ei	is like the *ay* in 'b*ay*'
ian	is like the *ien* in 'V*ien*na'
ie	similar to 'ear'
ou	is like the *o* in 'c*o*de'
uai	sounds like 'why'
uan	is like the *uan* in 'ig*uan*a' (except when preceded by *j*, *q*, *x* and *y*; in these cases a *u* following any of these four consonants is in fact *ü* and *uan* is similar to *uen*.)
ue	is like the *ue* in 'd*ue*t'
ui	sounds like 'way'

Examples

A few Chinese names are shown below with English phonetic spelling beside them:

Beijing	Bay-jing
Cixi	Tsi-shi
Guilin	Gway-lin
Hangzhou	Hahng-jo
Kangxi	Kahn-shi
Qianlong	Chien-lawng
Tiantai	Tien-tie
Xi'an	Shi-ahn

An apostrophe is used to separate syllables in certain compound-character words to preclude confusion. For example, *Changan* (which can be *chang-an* or *chan-gan*) is sometimes written as *Chang'an*.

Tones

A Chinese syllable consists of not only an initial and a final or finals, but also a tone or pitch of the voice when the words are spoken. In *Pinyin* the four basic tones are marked ˉ, ´, ˇ and `. These marks are almost never shown in printed form except in language texts.

Index of Places